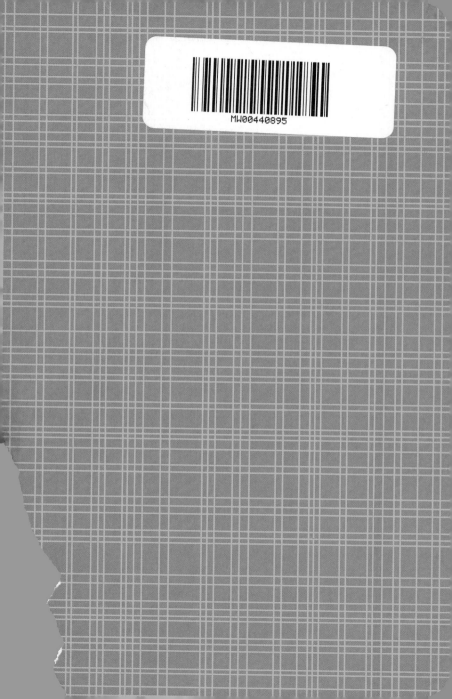

MW00440895

Ellie Claire
Hachette Book Group
1290 Avenue of the Americas, New York, NY 10104
ellieclaire.com

First Edition: October 2021

Ellie Claire is a division of Hachette Book Group, Inc. The Ellie Claire name and logo are trademarks of Hachette Book Group, Inc.

The publisher is not responsible for websites (or their content) that are not owned by the publisher.

Print book interior design by Bart Dawson.

LCCN: 2021939254

ISBN: 978-1-5460-1502-4 (hardcover)

Printed in China

APS

10 9 8 7 6 5 4 3 2 1

curiosities & (un)common sense from the BIBLE

WHAT HAVE I EVER DONE TO YOU?

60 DEVOTIONS BY ANTHONY RUSSO

Ellie Claire

To my wife, Rachael:
This would have never happened
without you.
I love you more than words can express.
I'm sorry I chew so loud.

contents

DiSCiPleS ArE FuNNY

*He said to them, "My soul is overwhelmed
with sorrow to the point of death. Stay here
and keep watch with me." ...Then he returned
to his disciples and found them sleeping.*

MATTHEW 26:38-40

The disciples were the closest friends and followers of Jesus who went on to begin the Christian movement and fundamentally change the world forever. But there were lots of bumps on the road to world changing.

For example, that time when they thought they were the miracle police:

> "Teacher," said John, "we saw someone driving
> out demons in your name and we told him to stop,
> because he was not one of us." "Do not stop him,"
> Jesus said. (Mark 9:38–39)

That time when they didn't listen as carefully as they probably should have, but instead took the opportunity to clarify who was the G.O.A.T. (greatest of all time):

> "Listen carefully to what I am about to tell you: The
> Son of Man is going to be delivered into the hands of
> men." But they did not understand what this meant.

It was hidden from them, so that they did not grasp it, and they were afraid to ask him about it. An argument started among the disciples as to which of them would be the greatest. (Luke 9:44–46)

That time when they thought they had to clarify to Jesus how sleep works:

"Our friend Lazarus has fallen asleep; but I am going there to wake him up." His disciples replied, "Lord, if he sleeps, he will get better." ...So, then he told them plainly, "Lazarus is dead." (John 11:11–14)

The disciples' presence in any story often makes me laugh. At times, they are undeniably admirable; at other times, alarmingly off-base. They are flawed people, enjoying a personal, intimate relationship with the God of the universe. Walking daily in close proximity to God in the flesh. They did not have the pedigree for this responsibility or the formal education for spiritual authority. And yet, God enters the scene and they are chosen.

One of the driving passions of the book in your hands is to encourage readers to engage with the Bible in a way they never have before, watching for curiosities that help form the whole of the story and reveal even the humorous side of God's character. Many people shy away from the Bible because we've been taught to "leave it to the professionals," that some are worthy of reading, studying, and interpreting this story about God, and others are not.

If you feel you are in the latter crowd, consider this: When it came time for Jesus to choose the individuals most responsible for sharing the gospel with the world, he chose a group of people who would later *mansplain* sleep to him.

God invites us all into a deeper way of understanding ourselves, each other, and the world, and does so knowing we will get things wrong, grow lazy or stubborn, get angry, and royally mess up.

The Bible is one big story telling us over and over that despite all evidence to the contrary, God believes in us. If we take the time to look closely at these pages, we start to see our own reflection. We hear a call beckoning us into the story.

Note: If the voice we hear leads us through a wardrobe into a magical forest, we're reading a different book. It's a common mistake. People do it all the time.

GET CURIOUS

Do you read the Bible as a dutiful habit, or do you appreciate the wonder and mystery and even the curiosities of it all? What can you do to create a habit of spending time reading the Bible?

The Talking Donkey

The donkey said to Balaam, "Am I not your own donkey, which you have always ridden, to this day? Have I been in the habit of doing this to you?" "No," he said.

NUMBERS 22:30

The responsibility of watching over children is not one to be taken lightly. When I worked in childcare at the Y, we staff members went through hours of training to be certified, then participated in ongoing training on topics from sanitation best practices to child psychology.

Despite my expertise, conversations like these were common in my kindergarten group:

> Me: "Excuse me, where are you going?"
> Anna: "I have to go to the bathroom. It's an emergency!"
> Me: "Oh…carry on."

> Me: "Billy! Give Steve his toy truck back!"
> Steve: "It's okay. I let him borrow it. We're sharing."
> Me: "Oh…carry on."

> Me: "Guys! What did I say about talking during homework time?"

Mikey: "Sorry, Adam was telling me about some recent tragedy he's dealing with at home and I was reminding him he has to stay focused on what it is he can control and not get lost in things that are beyond his control."

Me: "Oh…carry on."

Kids have a knack for reminding us to be more flexible about expectations. Apparently, donkeys do too.

Balaam was heading out on a trip with intentions God was not particularly stoked about. So God sent an angel with a flaming sword (the Bible doesn't specify it's flaming, but I imagine all angels' swords are enflamed) to block Balaam's way.

> When the donkey saw the angel of the LORD standing in the road with a drawn sword in his hand, it turned off the road into a field. Balaam beat it to get it back on the road. (Numbers 22:23)

Balaam must have taken classes on donkey management and assumed he knew better than the donkey in this instance.

Silly Balaam. Poor Donkey.

Then it happened again (Numbers 22:24–25).

And again (Numbers 22:26–27).

Finally, the donkey decided it was time to talk this out.

> Then the LORD opened the donkey's mouth, and it said to Balaam, "What have I done to you to make you beat me these three times?" Balaam answered

the donkey, "You have made a fool of me! If only I had a sword in my hand, I would kill you right now." (Numbers 22:28–29)

Obviously, thoughts needed to be expressed, on both sides, so the donkey reasoned with Balaam.

"Am I not your own donkey, which you have always ridden, to this day? Have I been in the habit of doing this to you?" "No," he said. Then the Lord opened Balaam's eyes, and he saw the angel of the Lord standing in the road with his sword drawn. So he bowed low and fell facedown. (Numbers 22:30–31)

Here's a man admitting that he didn't quite understand the situation as well as his donkey did.

Refusing to hear what God is trying to tell us along the way can land us on the business end of an angel with a flaming, double-edged sword. (The Bible doesn't specify that it's double-edged, but...)

God uses all kinds of things to point us toward a better way. Sometimes it's an unexpected word from a friend or a line of music or a piece of art.

And sometimes it's a donkey.

Get curious

How receptive are you
to what God might be telling you
about your plans?

God's Presence and a Good Policy

When you relieve yourself, dig a hole and cover up your excrement. For the LORD your God moves about in your camp.

DEUTERONOMY 23:13–14

My son is five years old and thinks it's very funny to answer questions with "poop."

"What do you want for your birthday?"

"Poop."

"Where do you want to go for lunch?"

"Poop."

"What did you do at church today?"

"Poop."

I guess there could be some truth to that last one.

He also likes to sing songs and spontaneously change out words for *poop.* Obviously, he has his dad's high-brow sense of humor.

Nobody warned me about this, but poop has become a larger-than-I'd-like-it-to-be part of my life in this season. Between our two young kids and our dog, roughly 20 percent of my day is dedicated to the safe handling and sanitary disposal of poop.

Biblical texts on this subject are some of my favorites, and although the passage about its involvement in bread-making is great (Ezekiel 4:12–15), I think this one is the best:

> Designate a place outside the camp where you can go to relieve yourself. As part of your equipment have something to dig with, and when you relieve yourself, dig a hole and cover up your excrement. For the LORD your God moves about in your camp to protect you. (Deuteronomy 23:12–14)

Imagine what sort of system existed before this policy was put into place. But I digress.

The image of God walking around the campsite, carefully stepping here and there so as not to sully the Birkenstocks is a great one. (I can't say for certain that's the type of shoes God wears, but I think we can all agree it's a pretty educated guess.)

I find the context of this law encouraging. *Keep this place tidy, because God is here.*

All too often, I imagine God on a throne in heaven looking down on me, like a commentator at a football game or a critic in a theater watching a movie. God is watching, judging, but God is removed from the action. I make God out to be the teacher of my online class who gives me critiques from miles away while I struggle with the online assignment portal and wonder if any of my work is actually making it through.

That's not the God pictured here. "God moves about in your camp." God is active. God is present. God is here.

As we go through life, particularly the hardest parts of

life, I think we all tend to ask why God is putting us through this. Why God allowed this to happen. I'm not sure if there are ever any totally satisfying answers to the question of "Why, God?"

But we can be confident the answer to "Where's God?" is *here*. On our good days, on our bad days, in success, in failure, in sickness and in health, for better or for worse.

God is here. God is close. God is with us.

So be mindful about where you do your business.

Get Curious

How does it change your perspective to know that God is everywhere you go? In what environments have you most strongly felt God's presence?

Bored to Death

Seated in a window was a young man named Eutychus, who was sinking into a deep sleep as Paul talked on and on.

ACTS 20:9

Nothing makes me feel more insecure than trendy coffee shops.

I like coffee. I drink a considerable amount of coffee every day. But when I walk into a cool coffee shop, I'm suddenly embarrassed about what I'm wearing, the way I take my coffee, how I invest, the type of music I listen to, and my thoughts on foreign governments.

I'm a fraud, and someone in here is going to call me out.

I don't deserve their single-origin, shade-grown, small-batch coffee.

The challenge for me when I'm in one of these rustic, industrial-styled palaces is to persevere through feelings of inadequacy, walk to the counter, and order like I know the difference between coffee beans harvested in Ecuador and those harvested in Ethiopia. The reality is, I bet most of those people don't know the difference between those beans either. Or any beans.

That's the problem with comparison. We usually compare an impossibly great version of "them" with the very worst version of ourselves.

You may be hesitant to share your thoughts about your faith, or anything for that matter. You may feel other people are better speakers, better storytellers, more dynamic in general, and they didn't start balding when they were nineteen (this is my testimony). You may imagine that if you share, someone might call you out, someone might be offended, or someone might not understand what you're trying to say. Or like, worst-possible scenario, you might bore someone to death. There would be no coming back from that.

> Seated in a window was a young man named Eutychus, who was sinking into a deep sleep as Paul talked on and on. When he was sound asleep, he fell to the ground from the third story and was picked up dead. (Acts 20:9)

If I were Paul, I would be reassessing EV-ER-Y-THING: *I guess my opening story isn't as hilarious as I thought it was. My three-point outline where every point starts with "T" isn't as captivating as I thought it was. Obviously, I'm not very good at this. Maybe public speaking isn't for me.*

Lucky for everyone, Paul was not much like me. What did Paul do? Paul brought the kid back to life, dusted him off, brought him back upstairs, grabbed a snack, and finished his sermon (Acts 20:10–11). Then he went on to spread the good news about Jesus all over the world and author most of the New Testament.

The point is, falling asleep during church is dangerous.

The point also is, if you *do* get the chance to share your faith, stick to your allotted time.

The point also *also* is, stop being so hard on yourself.

Speak up. Your voice matters. Don't let the fear of the worst-possible reaction from one person stop you from sharing your heart. And if someone does react that way, do your best to pick them up, dust them off, and finish your sermon.

You belong in this coffee shop.

And don't pay attention to their judgy eyes when you ask where you can find the half-and-half either. Coffee is bitter, and creamer makes it better. You know it, and deep down, they know it too.

Get Curious

Is there something you want to do, say, or share, but you're nervous about how someone might react? What will it take for you to give yourself permission?

ThE DaNcing King

*Michal daughter of Saul watched from a window.
And when she saw King David leaping and dancing
before the Lord, she despised him in her heart.*

2 SAMUEL 6:16

As with any great dancer, I have an arsenal of moves I mix and match as dictated by the vibe of the room and the flow of whatever the DJ may be spinnin'. One move in my repertoire causes dissension between my wife and me— "The Tummy Dance."

I admit it's a little riskier than my other dance moves. If I'm being honest, I primarily do it at this point only because my wife dislikes it so much and that is how husbands show wives how much they love them.

It's through this lens I approach the story of Michal and David.

Michal was King Saul's daughter. David felt unworthy of marrying the king's daughter, so Saul told him he could "earn" the right to marry her by delivering a hundred Philistine foreskins to Saul. (If you don't know what a foreskin is, ask your parents.) David, being the overachiever that he is, delivered two hundred (1 Samuel 18:20–27).

These two went through a lot together, and we learn (from the Bible, so you know it's true) that "Michal loved David" (1 Samuel 18:28).

Things were going great between these two lovebirds, until:

> Wearing a linen ephod, David was dancing before the LORD with all his might, while he and all Israel were bringing up the ark of the LORD with shouts and the sound of trumpets. As the ark of the LORD was entering the City of David, Michal daughter of Saul watched from a window. And when she saw King David leaping and dancing before the LORD, she despised him in her heart. (2 Samuel 6:14–16)

A "linen ephod" is essentially a sheer apron. David was dancing around in an apron, like I've been known to do while grilling hamburgers.

> When David returned home to bless his household, Michal daughter of Saul came out to meet him and said, "How the king of Israel has distinguished himself today, going around half-naked in full view of the slave girls of his servants as any vulgar fellow would!" (2 Samuel 6:20)

It seems David may have been dancing around in *just* the apron, which is, you know, a much more dangerous way to grill.

I've heard this story referred to in sermons expounding on what a wet blanket Michal was for being upset, and how great it was that David was dancing unashamed before the Lord. But I usually (tummy dance not included) tend to be a bit more Michal than David. I see people doing things I

wouldn't or in a way I wouldn't do them, and I judge. Usually silently, but judgy just the same.

I'm not talking about issues of morality, but about the way someone drives, or their preferred sandwich spot, or how they sing the lyrics on a slight delay during worship. I look down from my window all too often.

I'm quick to praise people for being authentic to their true-self, but the second that true-self rubs me the wrong way, I turn my sentiments around.

The David/Michal dancing fiasco was the demise of their once-loving relationship. They never recovered. Obviously, husbands' public displays of dancing can be pretty embarrassing (or considered modern art, if performed by yours truly), but it's not worth losing a relationship with someone you care about. Very few things are.

Get Curious

What is particularly irksome to you
in others? Are their opinions or practices
inherently wrong, or just different?

crazy in Love

Your teeth are like a flock of sheep.

SONG OF SONGS 6:6

My wife, Rachael, and I met at our church youth group when I was fifteen and she was sixteen. One of the first things I remember saying to Rachael was that she was as cool as a cucumber and as pretty as a flower. Then I drew her a picture of a cucumber flower, which was essentially Larry the Cucumber from *VeggieTales*, but with petals. In this one, early interaction, I gave away a few secrets about what Rach could expect from our relationship going forward. One, I don't draw very well. Two, I don't know much about botany. Three, I'm a regular swoon factory, so she'd better lock me down quick.

We dated for a long time. We stayed up until all hours of the night talking on the phone. (Praise God for free nights and weekend minutes.*) Inevitably I would start to nod off, and she would say, "Are you falling asleep? Do you need to go to bed?" and I, like a good boyfriend, would say, "No."

"Why would you say no?" a sane person might ask. Because I was in love. We say and do crazy things when we're in love. Rachael thought she was bothering me by keeping me up. I thought I was the luckiest guy in the world that she was talking to me.

Song of Songs is full of people in love saying crazy things

to each other, sentiments that live somewhere in the space between compliments and peculiar observations.

> His cheeks are like beds of spice yielding perfume. (Song of Songs 5:13)

Is this a compliment or a nice way to say someone has food on their face?

> Your teeth are like a flock of sheep coming up from the washing. Each has its twin, not one of them is missing. (Song of Songs 6:6)

This is definitely a compliment, albeit untraditional. Not enough people celebrate good dental hygiene when they see it.

> Your nose is like the tower of Lebanon looking toward Damascus. (Song of Songs 7:4)

As an Italian, I know better than most about the impact of a good strong nose. But if it's stuck pointing in just the one direction, then your partner may have slept wrong the night before.

> Your navel is a rounded goblet that never lacks blended wine. (Song of Songs 7:2)

Respect the innie or get outie.

Love changes everything. Something you might think is a flaw can be endearing to a person who loves you.

We can wrongly assume God only loves the good stuff about us. The best parts. Our proudest moments. But God also loves the things we are insecure about. Too shy or talk too much? Don't like the way you look? Too risky or too cautious? Whatever you think you're "too," God knows and loves that about you.

Whatever we think we have to change for God to *love* us, we don't. God thinks you're as cool as a cucumber and as pretty as a flower. As someone familiar with that terminology, praise doesn't get any higher than that.

*There was a time when we used to have to consider every literal minute that we talked on our cell phones and something called "roaming" was a real problem. Crazy times.

Get Curious

Is there something about you that you wish was different? Would changing it change the way God sees you?

If the Sheet Fits

But Abimelek said, "I don't know who has done this. You did not tell me, and I heard about it only today."

GENESIS 21:26

I avoid conflict. I avoid it at all costs. When people ask if I've seen a recent movie, my first instinct is to say yes, even if I haven't. To admit anything less feels like a twisted version of a conflict in which I do not want to engage.

I brought the conflict-avoidance trait, along with the rest of me, into my marriage. This is why it took me so long to be honest with my wife about something that was bothering me. I carried a heaviness with me for weeks. I thought and rethought about how to broach the subject. I considered contingency plans just in case the conversation went sideways.

Finally, the day came, and I told Rachael I was not fond of her biweekly routine of changing the sheets on our bed right before we climbed in for the night. I preferred to help put the sheets on earlier, so at the end of the night, we didn't have any additional chores between us and our heads hitting our comfy pillows.

I'll never forget her response.

"Okay."

That was it. She hadn't known I had a preference. It didn't matter to her. I'd dreamt up a nonexistent conflict.

Similar energy emanates from a story in Genesis about Abraham.

> Then Abraham complained to Abimelek about a
> well of water that Abimelek's servants had seized.
> But Abimelek said, "I don't know who has done this.
> You did not tell me, and I heard about it only today."
> (Genesis 21:25–26)

Abraham has been bothered for a while, and he's finally getting around to sharing his frustrations with Abimelek. It's been eating away at Abraham for days, weeks, maybe months. Abimelek is just now invited to the conversation.

We do ourselves and everyone else a favor when we invite others into the conversation sooner rather than later. We may not be able to perfectly articulate what's going on in our head, especially at first. But bringing supposed conflicts into the light is where we can see what's really going on, where we get our hands on the situations and deal with them.

I knew that if I was going to maintain a healthy, long-term relationship with Rachael, I was going to have to figure out ways to tell her how I felt. If I couldn't tell her about the sheet situation, how was I going to share my thoughts on the really important stuff? Like which kind of Cap'n Crunch is best. Let that sink in for a minute. If we never share how we feel, we could end up eating years of "Oops! All Berries." The stakes couldn't be higher.

It may seem like whatever it is that's bugging us is too trivial to address. We might think it's a lot of fuss to mention the specific brand of almond milk we prefer or how a particular nickname/term-of-endearment makes us feel. But it's

about more than that. It's about building trust with people we care about. It's about the courage to be vulnerable. It's about wrangling our thoughts before they run wildly out of control.

It's about exactly how many pillows are too many pillows on the bed. Which is the conversation I'm working up the courage to have next. Please send prayers.

Get Curious

Are you completely and lovingly honest about how you feel? Do you keep things bottled up and try to work them out on your own? What can you do to develop healthier habits about potential conflicts?

Just Jason

These men who have caused trouble all over the world have now come here, and Jason has welcomed them into his house.

ACTS 17:6-7

pisodes of *Law & Order* played on my TV a lot while I was growing up. Driving the plot of every episode was a cast of recurring characters—the detectives, the very suspicious early suspect who swears they didn't do it, the much less initially suspicious suspect who actually did it, and the people they interview along the way who have information about the case. The interviewees are the people I always loved—usually some guy loading a truck while Detectives Lennie and Ed asked him questions.

I loved these people, first of all, because they never stopped working. They were so committed to their position at the fish market or the truck-loading store that they wouldn't even take a break to discuss details regarding a missing persons investigation. (To be fair, those fish aren't going to ice themselves.)

I also loved these characters because of the juxtaposition between what a small part they had in the show and what a critical role they played in the investigation. They gave the detectives key pieces of evidence. More often than not, there would be no case without some random florist refusing to cease arranging flowers in front of her shop.

Because I love walk-on characters so much, I recognized one in the Bible when I saw him. He's mentioned in the book of Acts, but if you blinked while reading you might have missed him.

> So they rounded up some bad characters from the marketplace, formed a mob and started a riot in the city. They rushed to Jason's house in search of Paul and Silas in order to bring them out to the crowd. But when they did not find them, they dragged Jason and some other believers before the city officials, shouting: "These men who have caused trouble all over the world have now come here, and Jason has welcomed them into his house." (Acts 17:5–7)

Paul and Silas (the main characters in the story) are ministering in the city of Thessalonica, and Jason invites them to crash at his place. I love that Jason's role in this story made it into the Bible because the "Jasons" of the world are way too frequently undervalued. Particularly in American Christian circles, we get fixated on "lead" roles in the story: the preacher, teacher, missionary, evangelist, worship leader, celebrity—all the roles that carry a certain level of public visibility and performance. These characters are important, but movements are often powered by Jasons, by characters serving faithfully behind the scenes. People anonymously changing the world.

You may be hospitable, supportive, encouraging, and never be invited to guest-speak at Hillsong or the National

Day of Prayer gathering. It also just may turn out that teaching, preaching, and singing are not the most effective tools for convincing our communities how much God loves them. That distinction might belong to lives spent faithfully loving, caring, and serving their neighbors.

Don't believe for a second that your part is unimportant to the work God is doing in this world. You may not be the lead detective in this exhaustingly long-running cop show, but there isn't much of a case without you.

Get Curious

Has your spiritual journey been influenced by someone who wasn't on stage with a guitar or a microphone? What can the gift of hospitality do that the gift of teaching cannot?

Bearers of Bad News

*There is still one prophet through whom
we can inquire of the LORD, but I hate him
because he never prophesies
anything good about me.*

1 KINGS 22:8

A trip to the dentist was always a study in bad news for me. First the X-ray. "Bite down on this. It's going to hurt and you're going to gag, but it'll only take a couple of seconds. Sorry. Didn't get it that time. Let's do it again."

Then the X-ray results. "We've got to keep an eye on two teeth because it looks like they may be forming cavities, and the rest of your teeth definitely have cavities and we have to do root canals on most of them."

As unpleasant as these trips were, I couldn't help but feel pity for the poor dentist. All day, every day, he or she has to tell people that their steady diet of sugar and carbonated beverages is destroying the inside of their face and it's going to be very uncomfortable and expensive to undo the damage.

Nobody wants to be the bearer of bad news. Jeremiah knew this from experience. He had the distinct privilege of discussing the bright future of the current generation of Israelites:

For this is what the LORD says about the sons and daughters born in this land and about the women who are their mothers and the men who are their fathers: "They will die of deadly diseases…They will perish by sword and famine." (Jeremiah 16:3–4)

And painting a mental watercolor of the Israelites' utopian future:

Dead bodies will lie like dung on the open field. (Jeremiah 9:22)

And discussing the pleasant fate of those who accidentally survived the previously discussed incidents:

After that, declares the LORD, I will give Zedekiah king of Judah, his officials and the people in this city who survive the plague, sword and famine, into the hands of Nebuchadnezzar king of Babylon and to their enemies who want to kill them. (Jeremiah 21:7)

I hope that after delivering these devastating tidbits, Jeremiah gave the people some sort of gift to soften the blow. Like a painfully rigid toothbrush or a comically small container of dental floss. Something that would make the whole experience seem worthwhile.

Throughout the book of Jeremiah, God tells the prophet which version of bad news to give the Israelites, and a couple of times Jeremiah interjects how it's impacting his personal brand: "I am ridiculed all day long; everyone mocks me" (Jeremiah 20:7).

Bad News Bearer is a difficult job. It was a role that fell to the prophets in the Old Testament and frequently required them to deliver difficult messages to people in power. Isaiah had to tell King Hezekiah he was going to die (Isaiah 38:1). Micaiah (your guess at pronouncing it is as good as mine) gave King Ahab so many bad messages that Ahab said this about him:

> There is still one prophet through whom we can inquire of the Lord, but I hate him because he never prophesies anything good about me, but always bad. (1 Kings 22:8)

We may not always like it, but we desperately need Jeremiahs and Isaiahs and Micaiahs in our lives. We need people who can tell us hard truths.

Bad News Bearers don't have an enviable job. But we need them.

Get Curious

Do you have an open line of communication with someone who will tell you a difficult truth, and does he or she have your best interests at heart? When was the last time you told them how grateful you are for the role they play?

Struggles with Similes

Israel is swallowed up;...like something no one wants.

HOSEA 8:8

The Bible is a sacred book. It's an account of stories and prophetic messages that show God's love for all creation. God inspired the authors to write what they did, and what we have are their best attempts at communicating—through the language of their day—the spiritual truth God was revealing to them.

Some biblical writers were masters of visual imagery, expressing eloquently the message God had given them. Authors like the psalmist in Psalm 42:1, "As the deer pants for streams of water, so my soul pants for you, my God," or Isaiah in Isaiah 40:31, "but those who hope in the LORD will renew their strength. They will soar on wings like eagles."

Others were like Hosea.

Hosea's biggest struggle was with similes:

The Israelites are stubborn, like a stubborn heifer. (Hosea 4:16)

I guess "*stubborn* heifer" gets the job done, but it certainly lacks efficiency. If you have to say the thing is stubborn like the other thing is stubborn, I don't think you're metaphoring properly. Or simile-ing.

Ephraim's glory will fly away like a bird. (Hosea 9:11)

In the interest of fairness, I thought it necessary to highlight one of Hosea's better efforts. This one is so good, in fact, that it would later inspire an iconic Nelly Furtado track.

I think Hosea becomes aware that this is not his forte, so he kinda gets stuck on a simile he's comfortable with for a while:

They are all adulterers, burning like an oven. (Hosea 7:4)
Their hearts are like an oven. (Hosea 7:6)
All of them are hot as an oven. (Hosea 7:7)

Until finally it seems like he just gives up entirely:

Israel is swallowed up…like something no one wants. (Hosea 8:8)

Wordsmith or not, Hosea followed after God and wrote what he was inspired to write. I can't help but think of how many times I've paralyzed myself with qualification questions. I have an idea of what I want to do, but I hesitate as I wonder, *Am I strong enough*? *Do I know enough? Am I good enough?* The truth is, there is no metric standard whereby we decide who is good enough. Love God, love your neighbor, and pursue what you love. That's all you can do, and if you find yourself embarking on an adventure you don't feel qualified for, remember, if Hosea can write a book of the Bible, then you can do this.

A fear of embarrassment or failure can be another debilitating component in this experience. We can convince ourselves that enough preparation will eliminate these scary outcomes as possibilities. While I'm certainly not against preparation (to quote a poster from my middle school library, "If you fail to plan, then you plan to fail"), it's crucial to keep it in context.

The first time we attempt something (like creating meaningful similes) will likely not be the best version. But we may be amazed how much we develop through the "doing." Hosea's faithfulness to God changed him from a half-baked, simile-struggling writer to a fully-cooked contributing author of the most important Book ever written.

Which is why I always say, God is like an oven.

Get Curious

What are some big dreams or
aspirations you have?
Do those dreams seem too lofty for you?
Do they seem too lofty for God?

Are the Trees People?

Are the trees people, that you should besiege them?

DEUTERONOMY 20:19

Fussy has become one of my favorite words. As I write this, I have two young kids. They are growing and developing so much every day, but the constant flux of teething, picky eating, and ever-changing sleeping habits leave us with days when the kids are just fussy.

It's a pleasant word for such an unpleasant countenance.

When a kid is fussy, they are impossible to please. They're unhappy and not interested in any ideas you have to make their situation or distress better. When my youngest is fussy, he breaks out into a cry/whine and when you ask him what's wrong he says, "I'm crying." Fussy is as fussy does. As much of a pain as they are to deal with when fussy, we know it's not forever. *Fussy* is not an assault on their character or long-term potential. It's a description of a temporary condition. Get them a snack and a nap, and we'll reevaluate again after that.

I think we need to use this term more with adults, though. Everyone has so much going on as we balance home life, work life, relationships, dreams, goals, ambitions, and trying to drink enough water every day. Some days it's all too much, and we end up just plain fussy.

The unfortunate danger is that, like the parents of little kids, it's the people around us who catch the brunt of our fussiness. People at work, people in our family, or our friends.

A passage in Deuteronomy offers sound advice to anyone who finds themselves in one of those out-of-sorts, ornery, fussy days.

> When you lay siege to a city for a long time, fighting against it to capture it, do not destroy its trees by putting an ax to them…Do not cut them down. Are the trees people, that you should besiege them? (Deuteronomy 20:19)

"Are the trees people?" is one of my favorite questions in the Bible. It's a wonder to me why ATTP bracelets didn't catch on quite like the WWJDs did.

Biblical questions like this tell me God knew how fussy we'd get. When left to our own devices, we have a tendency to get frustrated and destroy everything in our path. We may not besiege cities, but limiting collateral damage is important in our everyday life so our attitude doesn't "besiege" the people we care about.

If I spill coffee on myself, what good does it do to take it out on my coworker? Is my coworker a tree…or a coffee-stained shirt?

If my dog was up all night barking, is that any reason to be cross with the local barista? Is my barista a schnauzer? (Side note, not the worst movie idea.)

When you have car problems, should you take it out on your civics professor? Although, depending on what kind of car you have, I could see how this one could be confusing.

It's best to stay focused on the true problem, even when we're frustrated. We'll get to a healthier place much faster if we take time to pause and identify what it is that's frustrating us.

It's probably not the trees.

Also, try having a snack and a nap. That never hurts anybody.

Get Curious

What was the last thing that set you off into a bad mood? Why was it so frustrating? Who is most likely to catch the brunt of your fussiness?

The Power of a Good Scream-cry

And he wept so loudly that the Egyptians heard him, and Pharaoh's household heard about it.

GENESIS 45:2

I was a very emotional kid. I cried a lot. Then I turned thirteen and committed to drying the tears up. I didn't think it was cool to cry.

Adolescence brought out the stone-like gargoyle in me. For ten years I only cried twice. Once at my wedding and once during the movie *My Girl* (even gargoyles are powerless against the line, "He can't see without his glasses").

Then I became a dad, and now I cry all the time again. Holiday commercials, reading children's books, the Olympics...All of it makes me cry.

Like me, Joseph was an emotional kid. One of the first times we meet him, he's a boy going to great lengths to tell his family all about his weird dreams (Genesis 37:1–11).

Dream-sharers are emotional people. They find their subconscious adventures dramatic and meaningful. They can't contain how they feel about them and decide the world needs to know every detail.

Emotional Joseph tells his family all about his trippy dreams—bales of wheat and celestial bodies included.

Eventually they got so fed up with him, his brothers sold him into slavery in Egypt.

A demotion and two promotions later, Joseph becomes the second most powerful man in the world (Genesis 41:41–43) and responsible for saving most of the world from a huge famine (Genesis 41:33–37).

Joseph's family back home runs out of food, so his bully brothers are forced to go to Egypt to beg food from *him*. Joseph recognizes them, but they do not recognize him.

A lot has happened since Joseph last saw his brothers, including a stint in the Big House (prison before the palace), a meteoric rise to power, and acclimation to Egyptian life, which probably meant the daily application of kohl eyeliner.

One might think all these experiences would make Joseph closed-off, difficult to read, and emotionally stunted. One would be wrong.

> He (Joseph) turned away from them and began to weep. (Genesis 42:24)
> Deeply moved at the sight of his brother, Joseph hurried out and looked for a place to weep.
> He went into his private room and wept there. (Genesis 43:30)
> And he wept so loudly that the Egyptians heard him, and Pharaoh's household heard about it. (Genesis 45:2)

Joseph is scream-crying at this point. Eyeliner is everywhere.

For a decade of my life, I operated under the delusion that expressing my emotions was a sign of weakness. Composure was the highest aim. Crying was unproductive, dramatic, and unnecessary. The truth is, crying can be absolutely necessary.

Expressing emotions is sometimes the only way forward through hard times. Everything is not made "okay" by *pretending* everything is okay. Jesus had such a short public ministry, and yet he thought it worthwhile to spend some of it in tears (John 11:35, Luke 19:41).

Hard times are not less hard and sad times are not less sad if we keep ourselves from acknowledging and responding to them appropriately. Withholding our physical response to emotions isn't only unnecessary, it's counterproductive. It hurts us, deepens the injury or pain, and distances us from others.

The good news is that one day there will be no more tears (Revelation 21:4), and in that same day, wolves and lambs will be friends (Isaiah 65:25). Videos of unlikely animal friends get me every time. Anyone have a tissue?

Get Curious

Which feelings do you resist? Which feelings are you most hesitant to embrace? How do you respond when you see others express raw emotions?

I Saw the Sign

*Gideon said to God, "...I will place a wool fleece
on the threshing floor. If there is dew only
on the fleece and all the ground is dry,
then I will know that you will save Israel
by my hand, as you said."*

JUDGES 6:36–37

I'm terrible at test-drives. I get that you're supposed to
take a car out on the road to get a real sense of how it runs
and feels and watch for signs that it's worth the investment.
The problem is, no one teaches you *how* to test-drive. They
teach you how to, you know, drive-drive.

Inevitably, I leave the car lot driving my standard three
miles under the speed limit, turn on the windshield wipers,
see if the air-conditioning is adequate, and fiddle with the
radio.

This is a finely tuned machine with over 30,000 moving
parts, meticulously engineered to safely transport me hundreds of thousands of miles, and I hang my decision on the
working ease of the AM/FM dial.

Gideon would have been similarly bad at test-drives.

God tells Gideon that he needs to strike down the
Midianites, but Gideon's skeptical and asks for a "sign."
What incredible display of power does Gideon request from
the God of the universe?

Gideon said to God, "If you will save Israel by my hand as you have promised— look, I will place a wool fleece on the threshing floor. If there is dew only on the fleece and all the ground is dry, then I will know that you will save Israel by my hand, as you said." And that is what happened. Gideon rose early the next day; he squeezed the fleece and wrung out the dew—a bowlful of water. (Judges 6:36–38)

To his credit, Gideon does ask for a sequel, although a bit of a derivative. This time it's the fleece that stays dry and the ground that's wet (Judges 6:39–40).

If I'm feeling confident enough to test God Almighty, doesn't it need to be a little more advanced than condensation manipulation? I would have asked God to do something really tough. Like connect a phone via Bluetooth.

Are we afraid to ask too much from God? Is that why we ask for silly things like a fleece to be wet or dry, or "our song" to come on the radio if we're supposed to get back together after a breakup? Those who claim no faith have occasionally pointed out how much easier their conversion might be if Jesus would just show up and explain the whole thing to them.

The message of Jesus is consistent. He always shows us a way beyond the tangible, the visible, the material. He teaches us what God is like and shows us how to live as a reflection of the divine.

Our requests for a sign from God must seem like trying to talk to someone about the inner workings of an innovative electric motor when they're only interested in whether the vehicle comes with a USB port.

And yet, throughout the Bible, God shows up for those who ask. The reality is, whether we can see it or not, God is always with us, always strong, always dependable.

The deeper those realities sink into our souls, the less we need to see a soaking wet sweater to believe they're true.

Get Curious

Do you believe God is with you today? Do you believe God is able to come through for you? How should that change your approach to crises or decision-making?

Say No to Calves

He ground it to powder, scattered it on
the water and made the Israelites drink it.

EXODUS 32:20

My basketball coach used to tell us mistakes were in-
evitable, but that we should do our best not to make
the same mistake twice. As devoted players, whenever we
missed a jump shot, we committed to not missing again. It
didn't always work, but it's the thought that counts. (Not on
the scoreboard, per se, but somewhere I'm sure.)

The Israelites had a different take on this whole con-
cept of replicating their mistakes. The first time they made a
golden calf was while Moses was on a mountain receiving
the Ten Commandments.

> [Aaron] took what they handed him and made it into
> an idol cast in the shape of a calf. (Exodus 32:4)

God hadn't explicitly written "Don't have other gods"
on a stone tablet yet, so maybe there was a little confusion.
Regardless, Moses returned from the mountain with a tablet
detailing, among other things, the official policy on other
gods. The Israelites were caught calf-handed and had to en-
dure a curious punishment for their actions:

> [Moses] took the calf the people had made and
> burned it in the fire; then he ground it to powder,
> scattered it on the water and made the Israelites drink
> it. (Exodus 32:20)

They could have learned from having to drink gold sludge. They could have learned from having a handwritten note from God saying, "No other gods." They could have, but they didn't.

Years later King Jeroboam decided, after some obviously subpar counsel, to give the calf thing another shot:

> After seeking advice, the king made two golden
> calves. (1 Kings 12:28)

For following such great advice, God bestows on Jeroboam this sweet sentiment:

> I will burn up the house of Jeroboam as one burns
> dung. (1 Kings 14:10)

Strike One: You eat gold sludge.
Strike Two: You're burned up like dung.
Let's leave it at that and never find out what Strike Three involves.

Following in the rich but mistake-riddled history of God's people, many of us struggle with the same issue over and over. We wonder when we'll be over this, beyond it, done with it. As if growing in our faith were a video game and we'd like to move to the next level.

My mom and dad were both alcoholics. It's part of my

family story. Personally, I only know one person who has experienced significant victory in a battle against alcoholism—my mom. She's not hesitant, even today, to say she's an alcoholic. She has been sober for years, but well aware this is her reality. She won't be defined or beaten by it, but admits it is a part of her story. She's smart, strong, kind, beautiful, my personal hero…and she is an alcoholic.

Because my mom decided to fight and continues to fight, she has made a wonderful life for herself. She's not repeating past actions that lead to regrets. She's a blessing to me, our entire family, and everyone she meets. We may find ourselves continuously fighting the same fight, but great things come when we don't give up.

And when we learn from others who have gone before us.

That's why it is best to avoid making golden calves, bronze calves, wooden calves, or Play-Doh calves for that matter, just to be safe.

Get curious

What led you to a place of regret? What environment were you in? Who were you with? What adjustments can you make to keep you from repeating a past mistake?

comforting Friends

*What they trust in is fragile; what they rely on is
a spider's web. They lean on the web, but it gives way.*

JOB 8:14-15

Michael W. Smith sang a now-legendary song with lyrics that propose a friendship can last forever, if Jesus is the Lord of the friendship. When you consider that in regard to some of your friends, it's a sweet thought. For others, it's, you know, something to think about.

Adult friends don't always have a lot of time to spend together, and often the limited time they do have is spent dealing with difficult situations. "Adulting" means that together we process job loss, sickness, divorce, deaths, the meaning of life, and jury duty.

Being a good friend in these moments is complicated. We want to do something, but aren't sure what will help. We want to say something, but aren't sure of the words.

Job's friends must have felt that way as they stepped into Job's unimaginably tragic story. If you're not familiar, Job is described as a blameless, upright man who was very wealthy and loved God. Job tragically lost all his kids, his livestock, his livelihood, and fell painfully ill—all very suddenly. His friends came to support him and approached with sentiments that we would do well to avoid when we console our friends.

> A spirit glided past my face, and the hair on my body stood on end. It stopped, but I could not tell what it was. (Job 4:15–16, Eliphaz)

As impactful as Eliphaz's pseudo-spiritual experience probably was (is he describing a spirit or is he describing a bad experience with deviled eggs?), it's not super beneficial when shared with someone in the midst of a personal tragedy.

> What they trust in is fragile; what they rely on is a spider's web. They lean on the web, but it gives way. (Job 8:14–15, Bildad)

Beautiful visual imagery here from Bildad, but encouraging as it is to think of falling through a spiderweb, exactly which step in the grieving process does it help one work through?

> But the witless can no more become wise than a wild donkey's colt can be born human. (Job 11:12, Zophar)

Maybe the intent here is to surround Job with solid, old fashioned, homegrown truth. I've yet to meet someone in mourning who wasn't dying for a good biology lesson.

Also, isn't it a little soon to bring up livestock in front of Job? C'mon, Zophar…

> Is there anyone like Job…? He keeps company with evildoers; he associates with the wicked. For he says, "There is no profit in trying to please God." (Job 34:7–9, Elihu)

This friend may have Job confused with someone else. A Joe or a Moe maybe?

Walking with good friends through difficult circumstances is daunting. Ultimately, nothing we can say or do will make the process easier or faster for them. It will take as long as it takes.

The best we can do is let them know they're not alone, be there for them, show up for them. We don't have to search for a magic word or story. Or stress over finding just the right worship song lyric to send them. We just need to be there.

The first thing Jesus did when his friends lost a loved one was show up and cry with them (John 11:35).

That's the kind of friend you want to spend forever with. I don't even want to spend a Monday with spiderweb guy.

Get Curious

Who is someone that has been there for you when you were going through a tough situation? Do you know someone going through a challenging time? How can you let them know they are not alone?

WWJD?

The Pharisees came and began to question Jesus. To test him, they asked him for a sign from heaven. He sighed deeply.

MARK 8:11–12

For as long as I can remember, I've felt a tremendous impulse to be nice. It manifests itself in weird ways.

If someone says to me, "Can you...?" I usually say yes before they finish. No questions asked. That's why I'm currently writing as I house-sit for two people's homes simultaneously. One that I'm working out of, and another that I'm keeping tabs on through a series of baby monitors.

Or if I accidentally make physical contact with someone, regardless of whether it's my fault or not, I apologize. You could run at me full-speed from thirty yards away and I would apologize for not anticipating your arrival.

When people bring up a movie or show I absolutely did not like, I will withhold my true feelings and point out an obscure thing I *did* enjoy about that show/movie. (What a great display of sound editing, am I right?)

I constantly try to avoid bumping into people both with my person and my opinions. My wife recently said, "Anthony doesn't want to interrupt anybody doing anything." I don't know that I've ever felt more attacked/seen.

I'm not suggesting this tendency is wrong, but the

pressure I put on myself to behave this way is unnecessary. I shouldn't feel bad for being bumped into or compelled to justify Nathan's terrible taste in movies.

In large part, I *don't* feel the pressure like I once did. Because, WWJD? That's right. What would Jesus do?

Jesus was a great guy. The best guy who ever lived. But you know what? He wasn't super nice all the time.

> Jesus replied, "How long shall I put up with you?" (Mark 9:19)
> "Hypocrites!" (Luke 12:56)
> As the crowds increased, Jesus said, "This is a wicked generation." (Luke 11:29)
> He replied, "Go tell that fox…" (Luke 13:32)
> "You foolish people!" (Luke 11:40)
> "Are you still so dull?" Jesus asked them. (Matthew 15:16)
> He said to them, "Do you still not understand?" (Mark 8:21)

Jesus overflowed with compassion. He was full of grace, love in the flesh. The Bible also records several moments (long before he said, "It is finished") when he was "done."

The takeaway for me is that it's not a sin to be frustrated, put off, or disappointed. It's part of the human experience that even Jesus knew and expressed.

What's worth noting is that after Jesus grew frustrated with these people, and let them *know* he was frustrated, he didn't give up on them. He wasn't hesitant to call Herod a fox (not a compliment, in this context), but he also didn't hesitate to give his life for King Herod.

The goal for all of us is to genuinely love people. It's not to rant, rave, blurt, condemn, judge, or ridicule. It's also not to pretend we are never let down, frustrated, or disappointed.

So, the next time you tackle me with a running start from the other side of the room, I will obviously help you up and find you an ice pack if you need it. But I will not apologize.

Sorry, not sorry.

Get Curious

What frustrates you the most?
What frustrations do you need to share
as they come up so those around you
know how they impact you?

welcome to the Neighborhood!

Select some towns to be your cities of refuge,
to which a person who has killed someone
accidentally may flee.

NUMBERS 35:11

You only get one chance at a first impression. This is particularly critical when meeting new neighbors. Depending on where you live, new neighbors can signal the beginning of a long-term relationship. You want to start this thing off on the right foot, consider an appropriate "welcome to the neighborhood" gift, and compose a few good jokes about "crazy Larry" a couple of houses down.

Here's the thing about neighbors. You may "know" this person for a long time, but your interactions may be limited. Aside from your first encounter, opportunities to chat may be reduced to when you're both taking the garbage to the curb, or walking your respective dogs. You may attempt to have a conversation but neither person can hear over the dogs barking, or the garbage truck growling.

I can't help but be curious about how the introduction scene goes in this neighborhood:

Speak to the Israelites and say to them: "When you cross the Jordan into Canaan, select some towns to be your cities of refuge, to which a person who has killed someone accidentally may flee." (Numbers 35:10–11)

Bob: "Hey, I just wanted to bring over this plant to say welcome!"

Jim: "Wow! Thank you so much."

Bob: "So what brings you to the neighborhood?"

Jim: "Well, the family and I were kinda growing out of our old place."

Bob: "Yeah."

Jim: "Also, the market is great right now."

Bob: "Sure."

Jim: "Also, you know, I killed someone."

Bob: "Same. So, have you met Larry yet?"

Do we think the Israelites came right out and asked about how and who they killed, which caused them to move here? Or did that information emerge organically over time? We do have an example of the unfortunate set of circumstances that can lead to this sudden relocation.

For instance, a man may go into the forest with his neighbor to cut wood, and as he swings his ax to fell a tree, the head may fly off and hit his neighbor and kill him. That man may flee to one of these cities and save his life. (Deuteronomy 19:5)

Whoever suggested this very specific example must have had a hard time finding partners for their wood-cutting adventures afterward.

The cities full of axidental murderers (see what I did there?) were safe places for them to retreat so unjust retribution would not be enacted on them by family members of the victims. From the beginning, God intentionally created safe spaces for everyone, protecting the vulnerable from those who would seek to harm them.

Unfortunately, this is not everyone's experience as they encounter the people of God. I've heard too many stories of people who were made to feel (intentionally or unintentionally) like an outsider or a burden or less-than by a church. Some are even victimized by a system that fails to provide a safe space for them. Everyone deserves a safe place among the people of God. There is nothing in our past and no decision we can make that can disqualify us from this. It's a God-given right, not a privilege.

Axes, on the other hand, are a privilege. So handle them with care and take them away from those who do not.

Get Curious

Is your church a place where you feel safe?
What can you do to make your church
a refuge for people in your community?

Help Wanted

Gallio showed no concern whatever.

ACTS 18:17

Wandering through Home Depot in search of a specific item can be a hopeless endeavor. You enter with one or two ideas of where that "something" might be—probably at opposite ends of the store. It's not in either place. You've now walked a 5K and still have no idea where to find sandpaper.

You give up your search and start looking for an employee to help you. One is assisting a guy buying painting supplies. Another is helping someone decide on a toilet. You stay on hold and browse through the toilet department for a moment but quickly realize those two are going to be at this for a while. Toilet selection is more serious than you thought. Your search continues.

Finally, hope appears in the form of an unengaged orange apron in the ceiling fan department. Your rescuer has a name. You describe what you're looking for and Brian's like, "Yeah, I don't usually do that section. Let me get Sarah over here." He radios for Sarah and then walks away. Sarah never shows.

You finally give up your search and drown your sorrows in two-dollar hot dogs from the vendor out front. You tell the vendor the whole story. He seems to really get you. You and the vendor follow each other on Instagram. Two years later, he's the best man at your wedding and everyone eats free hot dogs. Brian was not invited.

There's nothing worse than going to the wrong place for help. The Jewish people in Corinth knew what that was about.

Sosthenes and the Jewish leaders were not pleased with what Paul was teaching. They wanted help to stop him, so they brought their concerns before Gallio, the governor of the area:

> Gallio said to them, "If you Jews were making a complaint about some misdemeanor or serious crime, it would be reasonable for me to listen to you. But since it involves questions about words and names and your own law—settle the matter yourselves. I will not be a judge of such things." (Acts 18:14–15)

Gallio was a Roman leader and might not have been familiar with the intricacies and nuances of Hebrew law. If something were a more "serious crime," like let's say some innocent person was attacked and beaten in front of Gallio, then he would probably have felt more compelled to intervene.

> Then the crowd there turned on Sosthenes the synagogue leader and beat him in front of the proconsul; and Gallio showed no concern whatever. (Acts 18:17)

Then again, maybe not.

We'll all need help one day. It's not an if, it's a when. If you are not in dire need of help this moment, it's the perfect time to consider who you'd turn to if you were. We may have a list of people to whom we can send funny memes. We may have people who wish us a happy birthday on social media. But this is a different kind of relationship. Where would you go if you really needed help?

There's real strength in being vulnerable and asking for help, but it's important that we show discernment when it comes to when, where, and most importantly *to whom* we turn for help.

At least that's what my best friend, the hot dog vendor, always says, and he hasn't steered me wrong yet.

Get Curious

When was the last time you needed help or advice? Who did you turn to?

Great Expectations

She is like the merchant ships,
bringing her food from afar.

PROVERBS 31:14

Proverbs 31 is a chapter often used as a reference sheet for goals a woman should achieve. Although not a woman myself, even I know the gravitas that comes from calling someone a real "Proverbs 31 lady." It's high praise, to say the least. With descriptions like this, who could blame anyone for setting their sights that high?

> Her children arise and call her blessed; her husband also, and he praises her. (Proverbs 31:28)

What must a woman do to achieve this lofty honor? It's certainly not an undertaking for the faint of heart.

> She gets up while it is still night. (Proverbs 31:15)

First things first. You have to get up early.

> She is like the merchant ships, bringing her food from afar. (Proverbs 31:14)

That explains why you have to get up so early. You can't

grocery shop at the nearest grocery store. You have to go to Whole Foods on the other side of town. Got it. Wake up early and shop where you can't afford to live. What's next?

She makes coverings for her bed. (Proverbs 31:22)

Once you get home and put the groceries away, go ahead and change out the linens. No, not with the guest sheets from the hall closet. Make new ones. And 800 thread-count, if possible.

Speaking of making things and linens—start a small business.

She makes linen garments and sells them, and
supplies the merchants with sashes (Proverbs 31:24)

And get into real estate:

She considers a field and buys it; out of her earnings
she plants a vineyard. (Proverbs 31:16)

No sense making money without having a plan for it, and you can't have a plan for it without first doing some research. Why don't you become an expert on horticulture and vinification while you're at it?

The idea of aspiring to become a Proverbs 31 woman has been around for a while, but today it seems as though more and more people sit in that seat of aspiration. Home renovators, fitness models, lifestyle brands...More people are propped up for us to admire today than any day in history.

As with the Proverbs 31 woman, it can be a job just

trying to make sense of what these influencers' days must look like. More dangerously, the perception of their lives can make us feel inferior. How can celebs post daily latté art content when I can barely get out of the house for a nice latté once a month? What am I doing wrong?

Hidden stories lie behind every person we can aspire to emulate. Often, what we can see is hyperbole. It's a projected, inflated idea; an intentionally manicured brand image. Even authenticity can be commodified into a brand strategy. For some, it's more important to *appear* genuine than to *be* genuine.

We can't afford to get caught up in this standard. We are not failing if we don't work out like they do, eat like they do, look like them, vacation like them, or our house doesn't look like their houses.

Love God. Love your neighbor as yourself (Matthew 22:37–39). That's our standard.

Focus on that, and you won't need to stress if there isn't enough time in your day to make your own linens. A person needs a physics degree just to fold a fitted sheet. I can't imagine making one.

Get Curious

What higher-profile people are you following on social media? Do they encourage and inspire you? Do they make you feel like you're missing out or discontented?

Grocery Bags and a Goat

The goat will carry on itself all their sins
to a remote place; and the man shall
release it in the wilderness.

LEVITICUS 16:22

Every time I get home from the grocery store, I discover a new challenge. Can I get all of these bags into the house in one trip? Am I so pressed for time that I couldn't possibly make two trips? No. Have I nearly injured myself on this quest for unnecessary grocery delivery efficiency? Regularly.

I can't say why I feel this need to carry all the bags at once, but I'm sure it's somehow related to the voice in my head that suggests I politely decline any help from the bell-hop as I pull up to the hotel with four suitcases, three backpacks, a Pack 'n Play, and a case of water bottles. *I will carry all of this and pull every muscle in my arms to kick off my relaxing vacation, thank you very much.*

Leviticus is full of rituals and ceremonies, many of which involve goats. Of all the goat rituals, this is my favorite. These instructions are given to Aaron (the high priest) as part of the "Day of Atonement":

> He is to lay both hands on the head of the live goat
> and confess over it all the wickedness and rebellion
> of the Israelites—all their sins—and put them on the

goat's head. He shall send the goat away into the wilderness in the care of someone appointed for the task. The goat will carry on itself all their sins to a remote place; and the man shall release it in the wilderness. (Leviticus 16:21–22)

Aaron, spilling the tea of the entire community to this poor goat. What a picture.

There's no way the goat could look anyone in the eyes now. Not knowing what she knows. "Wilderness?" the goat says. "Sounds good to me."

Incredible and important parallels exist between the day of atonement and the life and death of Jesus. What I think is worth noting is that, from the very onset, the people of God were taught there were some things they were not meant to carry.

We wear ourselves out attempting to carry more than we should, both physically—when we try to move that glass coffee table because "it's not heavy it's just awkward"—and emotionally or spiritually.

God always has and always will provide a place for things we're not meant to bear—originally in the form of rituals and ceremonies, and now through methods that have less of a negative impact on goats.

Cast your cares on the LORD and he will sustain you. (Psalm 55:22)

Do not be anxious about anything, but in every situation, by prayer and petition, with thanksgiving, present your requests to God. (Philippians 4:6)

Cast all your anxiety on him because he cares for you.
(1 Peter 5:7)

Jesus said of himself in Matthew 11:28: "Come to me, all you who are weary and burdened, and I will give you rest."

Anxiety, shame, fear, and regret are all things you and I are not meant to carry on our own. Attempting to do so will leave us "weary and burdened."

Enter Jesus, like one of those abandoned luggage carts at the airport, already paid for, ready to bear the burden, asking us to lay our stuff down before we hurt ourselves.

We should take him up on that. If not for our mental health, at least for our rotator cuff.

Get Curious

What are you carrying, emotionally, right now? What are you worried about? What do you need to drop or roll onto God's much stronger shoulders?

Your Attention, Please

Listen, my sons…pay attention.

PROVERBS 4:1

My son just turned five years old. From the time he was born, I looked forward to this age because I thought it would be so great that we could talk and communicate. Newborn babies are fun, but they don't talk much, and when they do, they don't make a lot of sense. Also, I thought about how great it would be to just give him instructions and he would listen.

Funny story; he doesn't. Listen, that is.

I like to think it's his age. But let's be honest, kids don't like to listen to their parents at any age.

Just the other day, my mom told me something about a something retirement something I should think about.

And it's not just parents. We regularly don't listen to lots of people.

Not long ago I had a talk with my doctor about these somethings I should eat more of and these other somethings I should eat less.

You can associate the character trait with "Millennials" or "Gen Z," but the reality is, this has been a problem for a very long time.

This not listening has a long and rich history.

Solomon was one of the wisest and wealthiest people

to ever live. He was an expert on just about everything and wildly successful at whatever he set out to do. He authored the majority of Proverbs, a book of profound wisdom that still resonates with readers to this day. He presumably wrote the book, at least in some part, to pass on all of his God-inspired good advice.

His children, of all people, should eagerly and anxiously await these golden nuggets of guidance, and yet I can't help but hear a familiar parental frustration throughout the book:

Listen, my son. (Proverbs 1:8)
My son, do not forget. (Proverbs 3:1)
Listen, my sons...pay attention. (Proverbs 4:1)
My son, pay attention. (Proverbs 5:1)
Now then, my sons, listen to me. (Proverbs 5:7)

As smart as Solomon was, you would think he would have figured out the "I'm going to count to three" or "I guess you don't want a special treat" methods. (These are literally the only reason anything gets done at our house.)

It's a specific kind of exhausting when you don't feel heard, especially when you're trying to help. I don't know if anything is more deflating then when you express thoughts or concerns and the person on the other end either ignores or misunderstands you. In the worst form, these miscommunications can be interpreted as intentional. Conversely, an incredible amount of grace and mercy are extended when someone tries to tell you something, you miss it, and they reframe it and tell you again.

This is the God we meet in the Bible. A God who time and again point us toward love, health, and life. Essentially,

the entire Bible is God reframing for us, again and again, the story of redemption that's waiting for us. It's a message God never tires of sending.

I am grateful Solomon stayed patient and persistent with his readers, and I'm glad God does the same with me, because I'm not always the best listener.

It reminds me of that old poem where there were two sets of footprints in the sand, but then at certain points, there was only one. I assume because of the tide. I tuned out before the end, to be honest.

Get Curious

Who is the most patient person
you know? How do they impact the
people they interact with?

Interpreting Your Intuition

Jacob went close to his father Isaac, who touched him and said, "The voice is the voice of Jacob, but the hands are the hands of Esau."

GENESIS 27:22

One of my former high school classmates sent me a Facebook message. I hadn't spoken to him in years, but he asked how I was, talked about how cute my kids are, and wanted to catch up. I had reservations about his intentions. However, I'm usually up for talking about how cute my kids are, so I engaged.

Then it came out. An incredible opportunity. One I'd be perfect for. One where I could make anywhere from hundreds to hundreds of thousands of dollars a month. If I can get five people selling under me, and those people get five people selling under them, think about the potential!

Reality caved in around me. Did the guy even want to catch up? Did we even go to high school together? Are my kids even cute?? (Lol, that's crazy. Obviously, my kids are adorable.)

I had a feeling there was something fishy going on, but I'd proceeded anyway. That's a feeling Isaac knew well.

Isaac was facing his impending demise, so, as was his

family's tradition, he sent for his eldest son to pass on the blessing. Not wanting to bless on an empty stomach, he asked his son Esau to bring him some "tasty food" (Genesis 27:7) before they proceeded. Esau left, but (cue dramatic music) little did he know that his younger brother, Jacob, had conspired with his mom to steal the blessing. Jacob emerged into the room a few moments later instead of his older brother.

Poppa Isaac was immediately suspicious of the quick hunting outing (Genesis 27:18–20), but Jacob and his mom had anticipated they might need several steps for this ruse because they put goatskins over Jacob's usually smooth skin to make him *feel* more like Esau.

> Jacob went close to his father Isaac, who touched him
> and said, "The voice is the voice of Jacob, but the
> hands are the hands of Esau." (Genesis 27:22)

This begs the question, exactly how hairy was Esau? What type of personal hygiene regimen leads to a person being able to simply throw a goatskin on and pass as him?

The last test was a sneaky one where kudos go, again, to the costume department that dressed Jacob in Esau's clothes and sent him across the finish line.

> Then his father Isaac said to him, "Come here, my
> son, and kiss me." So he went to him and kissed him.
> When Isaac caught the smell of his clothes, he blessed
> him. (Genesis 27:26–27)

Isaac knows in his gut something is not quite right (and

it's not just the absence of tasty food). But he talks himself out of his concerns, blesses Jacob, and brings about years of family discord.

We're all more intuitive than we let on. The trick comes in learning to trust our intuition and the nudge of the Holy Spirit. While it is vital to be considerate and discerning, it's unwise to ignore a gut instinct completely. If you've got a notion there's something going on you can't quite articulate, it matters.

We can't afford to be distracted by quality costuming, tasty food, or keen observations about our adorable kids. We need to trust our gut about what's really going on.

Unrelated, but if anyone wants to sell Tupperware, let me know. It's a great opportunity and, just like our vacuum seal lids, I honestly think you'd be a perfect fit. Did I mention how cute your kids are?

Get Curious

What was the last strong intuition you had about something? How close were you to reading what was actually going on? How might you handle it differently the next time?

Be Nice to Birds

*If you come across a bird's nest beside
the road…do not take the mother with
the young…so that it may go well with you
and you may have a long life.*

DEUTERONOMY 22:6–7

People will tell you that all kinds of things will give you a long and happy life. Yoga. Yogurt. Hot yoga. Frozen yogurt. While all of these things are fine, I find it arguable at best that an ice cream imposter is something anyone should consider "good" for society.

The Bible mentions three specific things in association with the promise of a long and happy life (worth noting, none of them are frozen yogurt). First, live the way God has called you to live (Deuteronomy 6:1–2). Second, honor your father and mother (Exodus 20:12). And third, be considerate to mother birds:

> If you come across a bird's nest beside the road, either in a tree or on the ground, and the mother is sitting on the young or on the eggs, do not take the mother with the young. You may take the young, but be sure to let the mother go, so that it may go well with you and you may have a long life. (Deuteronomy 22:6–7)

One of these things does not seem like the others. So let's just come right out and address it. What does being nice to your parents have to do with a long and prosperous life? (Just kidding, Mom.)

As much as I'd like to take the situational bird commandment literally (aside from a couple of skirmishes with aggressive seagulls, I can honestly say "be nice to birds" is a commandment I have never even been tempted to break), there is a greater truth unveiled about the way God has called us to live.

The posture of the person in this bird scene is one of gentleness. Humility. It paints a picture that we will have needs, but we don't have a God-ordained right to recklessly take everything we want. The mother bird described here is sitting on her eggs/young. The person in the biblical scene has to carefully remove her. The human is bigger and stronger and has all the power in this interaction. But with this power comes the responsibility to be intentional and considerate.

You may suggest I'm making too much out of a poultry harvesting law, and you may be right (you usually are). But Jesus said he came not to abolish the law but to fulfill the law (Matthew 5:17). Jesus was the living, breathing application of these laws, and this is how Jesus addressed the world.

With all the power in every situation, he dignified those others shamed. He defended those others attacked. He honored those others disgraced. His actions were an outpouring of a Spirit that inhabited Jesus, and the same Spirit inhabits us.

We can choose to act the way Jesus would, whether our

choices are related to a contentious comments section, a text conversation with a relative, or when we stumble across uncooked nuggets on the side of the road.

Get Curious

When was the last time you found yourself in a situation of power? How did you treat others? The next time you're in that position, how can you use it to show extraordinary love and consideration?

BUSTED

*He took the things from the servants and put
them away in the house...When he went in
and stood before his master, Elisha asked him,
"Where have you been, Gehazi?" "Your servant
didn't go anywhere," Gehazi answered.*

2 KINGS 5:24-25

Calling in sick when you work at a doctor's office must be such a nightmare. You can forget about pretending to be ill. Even if you're actually not feeling great, your boss is a professional diagnostician of sickness who knows immediately if you're trying to stretch your seasonal allergies into a chill day at home.

If you do end up missing work, do you have to bring in a doctor's note? Do you have to go to a different doctor? It seems cruel to ask an employee to show up at work to get a note about missing work.

Gehazi finds himself in a similar predicament while working for Elisha the prophet.

A man named Naaman comes to Elisha to be healed of leprosy. Elisha instructs Naaman how he can be miraculously cured. Naaman (begrudgingly) does what Elisha tells him, and he's healed. Naaman returns to Elisha and offers gifts of gratitude, but Elisha refuses the gifts. Gehazi disagrees with that course of action and says to himself:

> My master was too easy on Naaman, this Aramean, by not accepting from him what he brought. As surely as the LORD lives, I will run after him and get something from him. (2 Kings 5:20)

Gehazi tracks down Naaman and accepts the gifts that Naaman offered to Elisha. Gehazi totes the gifts back to his house and then shows back up at work.

> When he went in and stood before his master, Elisha asked him, "Where have you been, Gehazi?" (2 Kings 5:25)

To reiterate, Gehazi works for a *prophet*. A prophet who, one chapter prior, literally raised someone from the dead (2 Kings 4:32–35). One could assume it might be tough to "pull a fast one" on someone so tight with God. Gehazi, however, attempts to do just that with this "rock-solid" alibi:

> "Your servant didn't go anywhere," Gehazi answered. (2 Kings 5:25)

Unsurprisingly, Elisha knew that was not true, and Gehazi was, indeed, busted.

> Elisha said to him, "Was not my spirit with you when the man got down from his chariot to meet you?" (2 Kings 5:26)

Being a Christ-follower can make us feel like Gehazi sometimes. We can't get away with anything. Initially, the idea that God is everywhere all the time is usually taught to kids as a comfort. Wherever we go, God is there. It definitely can, and should, elicit a warm, safe feeling.

But this is also true: God is aware of every decision we make. Every thought we have. Every motivation that drives us. Like with Adam and Eve, no matter what we do or where we hide, we can't "get away" with anything, because God sees everything.

The good news is, when we feel like lashing out as a reaction to a situation but instead respond with grace, God sees that, too. When we make even small improvements to take better care of our bodies, God sees that. When we educate ourselves on issues that affect people in our community, God sees. The work you're doing, especially the unseen work, is important, it matters, and God sees it.

Just like the guy who works for a meteorologist and tried to use bad weather as an excuse for being late, we can't get away with anything.

Get Curious

What choices are you faced with every day that no one else is privy to? What's a right choice you could make today that no one may notice but you and God?

New King Nerves

So, they inquired further of the Lord,
"Has the man come here yet?" And the Lord
said, "Yes, he has hidden himself
among the supplies."

1 SAMUEL 10:22

The most nervous I ever remember being was right before I proposed to my wife. My elaborate plan included dinner in the castle at Magic Kingdom, a ring wrapped around a rose petal, and an after-dinner surprise engagement party with our friends. I was very nervous about all the moving pieces.

It wasn't a cute, "Aww, look at him about to propose" kind of nervous either. It was a "sweating so much Rachael held my hand for a second and asked if I was sick" kind of nervous. A "couldn't find the person I was supposed to hand the engagement ring to, so I panicked and gave it to some random busboy" nervous. A "thrown off by an unanticipated princess parade right before the most important moment of my life and forgot how to take a picture" nervous.

Saul knew about doing weird things when you're nervous. He'd been anointed king of Israel by Samuel, but when the time came for him to be presented to his subjects, he lost it.

Finally, Saul son of Kish was taken. But when they looked for him, he was not to be found. So they inquired further of the LORD, "Has the man come here yet?" And the LORD said, "Yes, he has hidden himself among the supplies." (1 Samuel 10:21–22)

Saul was "hyperventilate behind the olive oil" nervous.

We find out one verse later that Saul was a tall man (1 Samuel 10:23). Imagine him not even totally hidden by whatever it is he was hiding behind. Nothing instills more confidence in the people you're about to lead then to be caught hiding like a toddler who doesn't realize his feet are showing under the living room drapes.

In fairness to Saul, Israel had never had a king before. God was their leader prior to this moment. That's a pretty tough act to follow. I can understand being a little intimidated by the task ahead.

But God had chosen Saul for this role, a fact Samuel reiterated right after the impromptu manhunt (1 Samuel 10:24).

Life is full of moments that feel too big for us. Moments God brings us to and we don't feel worthy to stand in. A presentation we're asked to give. A project we're asked to undertake. A child for us to raise. A person we're to mentor. A marriage proposal surrounded by Cinderella, Belle, and the rest of the Disney princess posse.

Whatever the moment looks like, God is here with us. God brought us here. God will give us everything we need to get through it. The nervousness that suggests we hide behind the olive oil jars is common, but the courage to step boldly into the moment God's brought us to is special.

Close friends gave me important advice on my most nervous day: "See that line where the sky meets the sea? It's a whole new world. Let it go, and at last, you'll see the light."

I'm still not totally sure what it means, but the marriage proposal went great. So, maybe there's something there?

Get Curious

What are you facing right now that feels too big for you? What insecurities have slowed you down in the past?
How can you lean into courage the next time you feel overwhelmed?

Second Chances

The men of Jericho built the adjoining section.

NEHEMIAH 3:2

I've never been very creative with LEGOs. I can build an airplane with guns out of LEGOs. A boat with guns. Also, I can do a car with guns. (Pro tip: If you put one of those longer LEGOs on the end, you can turn anything into something with guns.)

My LEGO specialty is building a wall. And, when I'm feeling particularly architecturally inspired, a wall with guns. I am eternally grateful for the innovation that is the LEGO kit, complete with neatly assorted bags and instructions. While I may not be able to freestyle a tub of bricks into a medieval castle, I can follow instructions pretty well. You should see me line dance.

Nehemiah is tasked by God to rebuild the walls of Jerusalem. Unfortunately for him, LEGOs hadn't been invented yet. His task comes with neither assorted bags nor instructions. Nehemiah does not know much about wall building, let alone the far more nuanced wall rebuilding, and that becomes apparent quickly in some of the decisions he makes.

By night I went out through the Valley Gate toward the Jackal Well and the Dung Gate. (Nehemiah 2:13)

Dung could work fine as a gate, I suppose, but rival cities will never stop lighting it on fire and ringing the doorbell to see if the Israelites try to put out the fire with their slippers.

And Hananiah, one of the perfume-makers, made repairs next to that. (Nehemiah 3:8)

Perfume makers. I can't imagine their profession would have a lot of crossover with wall building, unless you wanted the wall to smell nice. On second thought, if this section was anywhere near the dung gate, maybe a nice-smelling wall is not the worst idea.

In the end, Nehemiah accomplishes the task set before him. It's really quite the underdog story, but inside this great narrative is another story of redemption.

The men of Jericho built the adjoining section. (Nehemiah 3:2)

That's right, Nehemiah tasks the men of *Jericho*—the men responsible for the greatest wall mishap in history (Joshua 6:20)—to build part of the wall. Nehemiah puts into practice a timeless truth: When you're desperate, you'll take help wherever you can get it.

And an even more important truth, God believes in second chances. I use the word "second" loosely. God is more like a parent telling their kid this is the "last try" when we all know that kid is going to try until they make it. God offers us second chances time and time and time again. At every turn we are met by love, grace, and forgiveness. This is the story that God tells throughout the Bible, and it's lived out perfectly in the person of Jesus Christ.

Look at the relationship between Jesus and Peter. Peter deserted Jesus (Mark 14:50). Peter denied Jesus (Mark 14:66–72). Peter took a nap when Jesus specifically asked him not to (Mark 14:37). And this is the person on whom Christ said he would build his church (Matthew 16:18).

God always chooses the path of redemption over the path of least resistance, and that's the story God's inviting us to participate in. People who have done wrong. People who have dozed off at inopportune times. People who have disappointed us or let us down. People whose first wall fell apart when a couple of Jewish folks played their trumpets too close to it. We are putting God's love into practice when we offer them all a second chance.

Get curious

When did someone give you a second chance? How did that impact you? Is there someone to whom you can offer a second chance?

The Struggle Bus

Then Jesus said to them, "Don't you understand this parable? How then will you understand any parable?"

MARK 4:13

My initial day on staff with a particular church was at their staff retreat. The first speaker presented a devotional about what the church had been going through. He said some people were Green and some were Red. He talked about the importance of being connected in a Square or a Circle. Aside from my growing anticipation that the Blue Man Group might be performing at this retreat, I was completely lost and confused.

Did I ask for clarification on these terms? You bet I didn't. I wanted everyone to consider me part of the team. I didn't want them to know I was new. When you're on the team, you don't ask questions about stuff everyone else on the team already knows, right?

It turns out, these terms were tools the church had been using to simplify communication of larger concepts. They used colors and shapes (and llamas, for all I knew at the time) to convey nuanced ideas.

Jesus was a pretty unconventional teacher. He frequently taught in parables, through which he could convey spiritual truths using words and visual images people could understand.

Well…some people.

His disciples asked him what this parable meant.
(Luke 8:9)
After he had left the crowd and entered the house, his
disciples asked him about this parable. (Mark 7:17)
Then Jesus said to them, "Don't you understand
this parable? How then will you understand any
parable?" (Mark 4:13)

Jesus gets it that the disciples aren't exactly picking up
what he's laying down, so he takes a different approach. He
checks in with his students to see if they're keeping up.

"Have you understood all these things?" Jesus asked.
"Yes," they replied. (Matthew 13:51)

He also goes above and beyond to make sure they're
retaining and applying the material.

He did not say anything to them without using a
parable. But when he was alone with his own disciples,
he explained everything. (Mark 4:34)

Jesus was a living, breathing example of a new way to
live on this earth. Questions would always arise, even for
those closest to Jesus. Maybe *especially* for those closest to
Jesus.

The Church (the global, organized gathering of Chris-
tians) has a checkered history with questions. We have, at
times, done very well to address them, pray and meditate

over them, and learn from them. At other times, we have lashed out against the ones asking the questions (sorry, Galileo). Despite our checkered past, the biblical precedent is clear. Asking questions does not make you any less a part of the team. In fact, the team has always been built on question askers.

Ask questions. Ask people you trust. Do your research. Ask God.

You don't have to pretend that the first time you hear about a farmer walking through a field and tossing out seeds that didn't all turn out great (Matthew 13:1–23), you immediately comprehend powerful, nuanced, eternal truth. You can ask about it.

And when you do, you will be counted among a rich history of determined, sincere, and regularly confused Jesus followers.

Get Curious

How does this relate to that? When did this happen? Who was that? What does that mean? The next time you read the Bible or hear a sermon, jot down good questions, and ask away.

Good-Looking

But the LORD said to Samuel, "Do not consider
his appearance…People look at the outward
appearance, but the LORD looks at the heart."…
So he sent for him and had him brought in.
He was glowing with health and had a fine
appearance and handsome features.

1 SAMUEL 16:7, 12

You can't judge a book by its cover" is a sweet colloquialism most of us ignore.

One year, at my school's quarterly book fair, I got all hyped up on a book titled *The Attack* because the cover was a kid morphing into a tiger (at that time in my life I was collecting ceramic tigers. I wish I could tell you why). Long story short, a tiger on the cover does not, in fact, mean the book is awesome. My velcro wallet and I learned a tough lesson that day at the book fair.

Samuel, from the Bible, had to learn his lesson the hard way as well.

God tells Samuel to anoint one of Jesse's sons as the next king of Israel. Jesse had several sons, and Samuel did not know which one he was supposed to anoint, so he asked to see all of them.

Perhaps a bit of an impulse shopper himself, Samuel was inclined to anoint the first son he saw:

> When they arrived, Samuel saw Eliab and thought, "Surely the LORD's anointed stands here before the LORD." But the LORD said to Samuel, "Do not consider his appearance or his height, for I have rejected him. The LORD does not look at the things people look at. People look at the outward appearance, but the LORD looks at the heart." (1 Samuel 16:6–7)

Sorry, Eliab. You can get the serving bowls out of the high cupboard, but a crown remains just out of reach.

God teaches Samuel a clear and important truth. Don't focus on the appearance. This anointing should have nothing to do with looks. It should be like auditions on *The Voice*. Samuel should not even turn his chair around until he decides he is ready to anoint the contestant.

All of Jesse's other sons parade through. Samuel doesn't push his button for any of them. Jesse's youngest son emerges as the last option (by process of elimination, likely the future king), and what element of this young man's spirit does Samuel immediately document? His generosity? His patience? His kindness?

> He was glowing with health and had a fine appearance and handsome features. (1 Samuel 16:12)

It's his strong jawline. Come on, Samuel. Have you learned nothing?

We constantly make decisions based on what we can measure, what we can see or count. What the Bible repeats as a theme is that there is more going on than meets the eye. The boy Samuel anointed that day was David, who would become King David, a man the Bible later described as a man after God's own heart (Acts 13:22). David would go on to become a prolific biblical author (he wrote about half of the Psalms), and probably the most recognized and beloved leader of the Jewish people.

God saw all of that in the "anointing" moment while Samuel only saw high cheekbones.

Whether it's choosing a life partner, a college major, or a book at the book fair, making good decisions can be hard. The good news is that we do not have to make these decisions alone. We make these decisions alongside a God who sees what we can't see and promises that if we ask it will be given and if we seek then we will find (Matthew 7:7).

Also, as in Samuel's case, avoid tall people. They are obviously not to be trusted.

Get Curious

What was the last big decision you made? Did you spend concentrated time praying about it?

It's a Frog-Eat-Frog World

The frogs came up and covered the land.
But the magicians did the same things by
their secret arts; they also made frogs
come up on the land of Egypt.

EXODUS 8:6-7

Making giant boats disappear, pulling rabbits out of hats, wearing a tuxedo to work every day...I have total respect for professional magicians. While catching a bullet between your teeth, escaping from a straitjacket, or freezing yourself in a block of ice is certainly impressive (Well, impressive to you and me. David Blaine refers to this trifecta as "Tuesday"), you have to question the usefulness of all this stuff. I mean, you don't have to survive in a frozen block of ice if you never freeze yourself in a block of ice.

When Aaron and Moses show up intent on setting the Israelites free and causing problems for the Egyptians, Pharaoh continuously turns to his magicians for solutions. The first instance is when Aaron turns his walking staff into a snake and the magicians, ignoring the more obvious choice of conjuring a magical snake-eating mongoose, decide to fight fire with fire in the form of a snake of their own (Exodus

7:11–12). Unfortunately for them, they created inferior snakes that were eventually swallowed by Aaron's snake (Exodus 7:12). You know what they say: don't bring a constrictor to a cobra fight.

Later, the magicians are called in after Moses and Aaron had turned all the water in Egypt to blood. What was their answer to stop the literal and proverbial bleeding? They turned more water into blood (Exodus 7:21–22).

Pharaoh, like any good coach or snack mom, refuses to give up on his team and gives them another chance when Moses and Aaron cause frogs to come up and cover the land. Compared to the other issues, getting rid of frogs seems pretty doable. It could probably even be done without magic, through a concerted community effort. Eliminating even just one frog would be a step in the right direction. The magicians, however, take a different path and instead address the frog overpopulation problem by making more frogs (Exodus 8:6–7). This is literally like calling exterminators about removing a possum from your attic and instead they bring a family of possums so the original possum won't be lonely.

Accentuating the positives, Pharaoh's magicians *have* been able to somewhat replicate plagues of God, which is pretty impressive (albeit useless to the people on whom the plagues were inflicted). That is, until:

> All the dust throughout the land of Egypt became gnats. But when the magicians tried to produce gnats by their secret arts, they could not. (Exodus 8:17–18)

Anyone who steps outside after it's just rained can make gnats appear, but not these celebrated magicians.

93

They specialize exclusively in blood-water, frogs, and mild-tempered staff-snakes. You could certainly argue that this is the most helpful the magicians have been in dealing with a problem. By not producing gnats, they at least didn't make the problem worse, which is—you know—something.

The world is not made better and problems are not solved by people striving to prove they're as good as anybody else. Unfortunately, any sort of validation achieved by these efforts will always come up empty. If you don't believe you're good enough, no one will be able to convince you otherwise.

The moment we make an aim of proving ourselves an equal to someone else on any level—professionally, financially, relationally, magically—we rob our own life of its unique joys. Be unapologetically, relentlessly, exactly the person God made you. Don't strive to be somebody else.

Bring something new to the table. We're all set on the frog front.

Get Curious

Are you sometimes jealous of the success of others? Do you know what God thinks about you? (If you're not sure, read and consider carefully Psalm 139:13–16, 1 Peter 2:9, Ephesians 2:10, 1 John 3:1.)

Are You Drunk?

Hannah was praying in her heart, and her lips were moving but her voice was not heard. Eli thought she was drunk.

1 SAMUEL 1:13

My mom was driving me to my friend Dino's house. I was twelve or thirteen at the time. On our way, she asked a bunch of questions, and I responded with exclusively one- or two-word answers.

Somewhere within that seven-minute drive to Dino's house, my mom had enough of my short answers, and asked bluntly, "Are you on drugs? You know, this is how people act when they're on drugs."

There I was, minding my own business, excited to play video games at Dino's, and now I was being interrogated on grounds of suspected drug use! I wasn't on drugs. I had never even seen a drug.

Whatever I said in response, it eased her mind enough that she still let me go to Dino's, where the only mushrooms present were the ones I used to get high scores in Super Smash Bros and smoke him at Mario Kart. (I'm starting to realize how some of these terms may have also contributed to my mom's suspicions.)

It's a strange phenomenon, being accused of something

so off-base like that. Hannah experienced it at the hands of Eli (the high priest) as she prayed in the temple:

> As she kept on praying to the LORD, Eli observed her mouth. Hannah was praying in her heart, and her lips were moving but her voice was not heard. Eli thought she was drunk and said to her, "How long are you going to stay drunk? Put away your wine." "Not so, my lord," Hannah replied, "I am a woman who is deeply troubled. I have not been drinking wine or beer; I was pouring out my soul to the LORD." (1 Samuel 1:12–15)

If Eli thinks people get quieter when they're drunk, he's clearly not been around very many drunk people. Poor Hannah. One minute she was minding her business, pouring out her soul to the Lord, and the next she was headed straight for a field-sobriety test.

Far too often we make assumptions, formulate opinions, and prepare suggestions based on partially assembled, empirical evidence. Just like Eli, we see the problem before we see the person.

But we have such an opportunity to heal, encourage, and affirm in these moments. I'm living proof of that. My mom decided to leave my dad when the situation became dangerous for us both. We had few options for places to turn. Our local church took us in. The church housed us. Fed us. Supported us. Loved us. In our most desperate time, the church showed up.

The opportunity for this kind of impact is open to us every time someone walks through the doors of the church in their hour of need. Like Eli did, we can assume everyone is tipsy, or we can assume the best about them and extend the timeless, life-altering love of Christ.

After the confusion is dispelled, Eli blesses Hannah. As she leaves, she shows us one more timeless, practical truth that Eli, Hannah, my mom, and Dino all agree on:

> Then she went her way and ate something, and her face was no longer downcast. (1 Samuel 1:18)

The right snack can turn any day around.

Get Curious

Do you assume the best or the worst about people when you first meet them? Do you give people the benefit of the doubt? What would change if you did?

WISh LISts

But the people refused to listen to Samuel.
"No!" they said.

1 SAMUEL 8:19

When I turned seven, my mom and I went out for my birthday dinner. Mom asked what I wanted to order, and I told her, "Shepherd's pie." Knowing my tastes well, she said I wouldn't like it and insisted, "That isn't like regular pie."

She had to be lying. I'd only recently learned her "real name" wasn't even Mom. It would be very on-brand for her to also keep from me a perfect dish that presented dessert as a dinner, creating space for an additional, after-pie dessert.

In one last effort to save me from myself, she warned that if I ordered it, she would force me to eat every last bite.

Sure, Mom. Like I'm gonna have a hard time eating my "dinner pie."

Fast-forward. I'm sobbing in a public restaurant because I'm so grossed out (and betrayed) by my dinner. Happy birthday to me.

How was I supposed to know what an expert my mom was on Irish cuisine?

The ancient Israelites would have known exactly what I'm talking about. They really wanted a king, because all the other countries had a king. (Also, because without one, their chess games were endless.)

Samuel gives them a glimpse into "life with a king":

> He said, "This is what the king who will reign over
> you will claim as his rights…He will take the best of
> your fields and vineyards and olive groves and give
> them to his attendants. He will take a tenth of your
> grain and of your vintage and give it to his officials
> and attendants…He will take a tenth of your flocks,
> and you yourselves will become his slaves. When that
> day comes, you will cry out for relief from the king you
> have chosen, but the LORD will not answer you in that
> day." (1 Samuel 8:11, 14–15, 17–18)

What does Samuel know? So what if he "talks to God"? That's not the king the Israelites imagined. Their king would ride in parades and knight people and grow crops of candy in the fields.

The Israelites respond much in a way that would make my eloquently stubborn seven-year-old self proud.

> But the people refused to listen to Samuel. "No!" they
> said. (1 Samuel 8:19)

After much persistence, the Israelites got their king. And everyone loved him and he loved everyone and they all lived happily ever after.

Not exactly.

The Israelites had a couple of good kings, but suffered through a long series of bad ones, which eventually led to their being exiled from their land and taken into captivity.

Sometimes I think the greatest gift God gives us is to

keep us from what we think we want. The desires are so real, so palpable, but are formed without knowing the full picture.

We desperately want that job because of the salary, but don't see it comes with an incredible level of stress. We want that house because of the neighborhood, but don't see cracks in the foundation. We want a relationship with that person, but don't hear what it sounds like when they chew.

We can trust God knows the desires of our hearts even better than we do, and when we don't get what we so desperately want, it's usually because it comes with peas.

God and your mom both know you don't like peas.

Get Curious

What desire did you receive that didn't live up to your expectations? What didn't you get that you're thankful you avoided? How have your desires changed as you've grown and matured?

The Omnipotent Optometrist

This is what the Sovereign LORD showed me:
a basket of ripe fruit. "What do you see, Amos?"
he asked. "A basket of ripe fruit," I answered.

AMOS 8:1-2

Getting a driver's license is an exciting experience. Riding around with your friends, going wherever you please, trying to guess what those warning lights on the dashboard mean. It's the beginning of a brand-new era of opportunity.

I took Driver's Ed at my high school, so when I went to the DMV to get my learner's permit (the first step toward getting my license), I just had to pass the eye exam. To pass this exam, all I had to do was look into a little machine and report what letters I saw. The man who was giving me my eye exam was not nearly as excited as I was about this process but dutifully went through the motions for me.

He loaded up the eye exam machine, but when I looked in, there was nothing there. I told him that he made a mistake and there were no letters in the machine. He said the letters were in there. I said they weren't. He said they were. This went on for a bit. He finally relented and put different letters in the machine, and I looked again. Still nothing. I suggested maybe the machine was broken. He said it wasn't. I said it was. This went on for a bit.

A few days later I went to the eye doctor. When given a similar test, I could hardly make out anything below the big "E" on the letter pyramid in the office. This only confirmed the diagnosis that my unenthusiastic DMV friend had already given. I desperately needed glasses.

What was supposed to be a day celebrating my new-found independence, as I clutched the keys to the family car, was instead a day when I realized I would be super dependent on these two pieces of glass anchored to my ears. (Although the way most of my fellow Floridians drive, I would have fit right in if I'd driven myself home that day.)

It's an unsettling experience to identify something when you don't even know what you're looking at. An experience that—once you accept it's not a machine malfunction—immediately fills you with self-doubt. It makes you wonder what else you might be missing. It makes you question your capabilities. This is why I'm encouraged by these accounts of prophets and God in the Old Testament.

> The LORD showed me two baskets of figs placed in front of the temple of the LORD…Then the LORD asked me, "What do you see, Jeremiah?" "Figs," I answered. (Jeremiah 24:1–3)

> This is what the Sovereign LORD showed me: a basket of ripe fruit. "What do you see, Amos?" he asked. "A basket of ripe fruit," I answered. (Amos 8:1–2)

I bet Jeremiah and Amos got *their* learner's permits on the first try.

Too often I stress about missing what God is trying to teach me because it's buried in a podcast I don't listen to, or it's tucked behind a Hebrew word I don't know, or in the breakout session of a conference I haven't attended.

In stark contrast, we have these passages where God reveals truth directly to people, right in front of their faces, using ordinary things they can recognize. While other traditions have depicted a divine being that requires disciples to pass certain checkpoints in order to ascertain truths, the Bible paints a beautiful picture of a God who is willing to reveal truths using our favorite snacks.

It's just, with some of us, God has to hold the snacks a little closer so we can see them.

Get Curious

Do you think God can reveal truth to you? Is there something you think you need to accomplish or achieve to gain that distinction? Let that idea go.

True Friends Don't Stab You in the Gut

He presented the tribute to Eglon king of Moab,
who was a very fat man.

JUDGES 3:17

We don't know much about Ehud from the book of Judges. We know he was left-handed (Judges 3:15). And we know he was incredibly brave.

> Now Ehud had made a double-edged sword about a cubit long, which he strapped to his right thigh under his clothing. (Judges 3:16)

(Seriously, there had to be a safer way to transport that.)

We know that Ehud was to deliver the Israelites from the hand of Eglon, king of Moab, whom we also know little about. Eglon conquered the Israelites, ruled over them for eighteen years (Judges 3:13–14), and we also get this little factoid:

> Eglon king of Moab...was a very fat man. (Judges 3:17)

This sets up our showdown. The left-handed, groin-sworded Ehud versus the large and in-charge Eglon. What happens next plays out like your classic Hollywood plot, Ehud playing the role of secret agent.

> He himself went back to Eglon and said, "Your
> Majesty, I have a secret message for you."
> (Judges 3:19)

Eglon immediately trusts Ehud completely, and sends away all his closest companions (Judges 3:19).
And then this:

> Ehud reached with his left hand, drew the sword
> from his right thigh and plunged it into the king's
> belly. Even the handle sank in after the blade, and his
> bowels discharged. Ehud did not pull the sword out,
> and the fat closed in over it. (Judges 3:21–22)

The tale of Eglon continues, unfortunately, as Ehud escapes and Eglon's crew stands outside the king's chamber, wondering how long this secret-sharing session is going to last.

> After he had gone, the servants came and found the
> doors of the upper room locked. They said, "He must
> be relieving himself in the inner room of the palace."
> They waited to the point of embarrassment. (Judges
> 3:24–25)

I have to imagine there were certain aromas that led them to believe Eglon was relieving himself and caused them to wait "to the point of embarrassment" before forcing

their way into the room. A spy, a dangerous secret, and it all ends in a big poopy mess. Like I said, just your typical Hollywood blockbuster.

As unlikely as it may seem, I think we can learn an important life lesson from the demise of King Eglon.

When we meet new, interesting people, we're tempted to give them undue influence and access to our lives. Whether it's a new friend, a romantic interest, or a personality on social media—new people are fascinating. They're so full of backstory that we don't know and experiences we haven't had. Every opinion they hold, every preference, every suggestion they make can feel like pure gold, and some of their influence can be beneficial. However, as Eglon displayed, too much trust given too quickly can be dangerous.

Trust should be earned. It's built over time. It's established as you truly get to know someone's story, their dreams, their motivations. Until we have some of these pieces to the puzzle, we can't be sure if what they have to offer is a new song for our playlist or a hidden shiv we'll never see coming. The people we trust the most should have some history with us, and we should have some history with them.

And they should know to check on us if we've been in the bathroom too long.

Get Curious

At this moment in your life,
whose opinion do you value most?
Is this someone who knows you well
and has your best interests at heart?

up for Negotiation

*I will let you bake your bread over cow dung
instead of human excrement.*

EZEKIEL 4:15

I have done some very passionate negotiating with God over the years. The most common example would be promises I made if God would get me through a tight spot. These negotiations were usually conducted while the test I had not studied for was being handed out. I promised I would do my devotions every morning. I would pray more. I would memorize Scripture. I would stop listening to secular music when my parents weren't around. Anything and everything was on the table.

The Bible is full of people eager to engage in divine negotiations.

Like when Abraham asked if God would really and truly "sweep away the righteous with the wicked" if there were fifty righteous people in Sodom and Gomorrah (Genesis 18:24). God agreed to spare Sodom and Gomorrah for fifty righteous people, and an emboldened Abraham pushed even further:

> What if the number of the righteous is five less than fifty? Will you destroy the whole city for lack of five people? (Genesis 18:28)

I love that line, because I feel like it's the same logic that usually ends with me being upsold on something. Am I really going to not get bacon on my burger, just because it's five dollars more?

Six rounds of negotiations later, Abraham talked God down to ten righteous people (Genesis 18:32).

On another occasion, God had a message for the Israelites about their impending difficulties and, to illustrate it, told Ezekiel to bake bread and use "human excrement" to fuel his fire. Ezekiel (shockingly) was not keen on this idea and negotiated his way to one of my favorite verses in the whole Bible:

> Very well...I will let you bake your bread over cow dung instead of human excrement. (Ezekiel 4:15)

Obviously, this deal seems to stink either way, but it is certainly of note that God gave a direction to Ezekiel that was adjusted based on Ezekiel's "preference."

Then there's the time when, while alone in the desert, Jacob engaged God in the less popular, cage-match style of negotiation, until finally declaring, "I will not let you go unless you bless me" (Genesis 32:26). God does, eventually, bless Jacob and gives him a new name (Genesis 32:28).

Jesus also negotiated with God, moments before he was to be crucified:

> My Father, if it is possible, may this cup be taken from me. Yet not as I will, but as you will. (Matthew 26:39)

Jesus went back to the negotiation table a second

time (v. 42), but this particular issue was nonnegotiable. Sometimes that's the case. But how fascinating that Jesus—God in the flesh—thought it worthwhile to express to God that he'd prefer it not be this way.

For a long time, my default, blurry image of prayer had me laying down a request at the feet of a giant sky throne to a giant sky god who might or might not consider my request because there were tons of people in line behind me laying down similar requests. But that's not the God in these stories. The God in these stories is present, active, and listening.

We don't always get the answer we request. Jesus didn't get the answer he requested. But even if the answer is not the one we want, the response does not come from a cold, distant, and silent god. The answer comes from a God who loves us enough to sit at the negotiation table and look us in the eye when we talk.

Or suplex us to the mat, you know, depending on our negotiation style.

Get Curious

When you talk to God, how comfortable are you about being honest?
How much does comfortability in your communication depend on a healthy relationship with God?

Bald Guys and Bears

As he was walking along the road, some boys
came out of the town and jeered at him.
"Get out of here, baldy!" they said.
"Get out of here, baldy!"

2 KINGS 2:23

Going bald is no fun. One day, you've got your hair, and everything's great. Then, with very little warning, you wake up, and your hair has packed its belongings and left. No note. No nothing.

It's hard to trust again after you go bald. The feelings of abandonment are real, and they sting. When I was eighteen years old, I had long, flowing hair. Now, in my early thirties, I'm racing toward Vin Diesel status.

Making fun of bald people is cruel, and it always has been, as evidenced by the 2 Kings 2:23 reference to boys calling Elisha "baldy." While I can definitely understand what Elisha must have been feeling at this moment, there's still a big part of me that thinks this may have been an over-reaction:

> He turned around, looked at them and called down
> a curse on them in the name of the LORD. Then two
> bears came out of the woods and mauled forty-two of
> the boys. (2 Kings 2:24)

Wait. Forty-two of them? I pictured a small group of punks, a sandlot gang. But that's more like an entire tribe of Lost Boys.

When a book bears a title referring to funny, humorous, or curious parts of the Bible, this particular story is bound to show up. When I ask friends to name their favorite funny Bible story, this wins the vote every time. While it would feel disingenuous not to include this passage, if I'm being honest, I'm not sure exactly what to take away from it.

I do know this: I have often wished bad things on people who have hurt me. Most of the time, those bad things never happened (I'm obviously not as spiritual as Elisha), and if bad things *did* actually happen to those people, I didn't feel good about it.

Maybe you've experienced something similar. You leave a job or team or relationship and instinctively (and more than a little immaturely) want the worst for that person or those people. As it turns out, seeing people miserable rarely makes anyone feel any better. It doesn't relieve our pain and makes us cringe with remorse.

Fighting the desire isn't easy. Revenge comes all too naturally. The compulsion to be vindicated is strong. Our need for affirmation can make our thoughts drift toward bitterness or retaliation. I'm trying to do better about making sure my thoughts toward others mirror the thoughts God has for me. God wants me to thrive. God wants what's best for me. God wants me to be confident. I should want these things for other people.

That's exactly why no one should make fun of bald people. If it's Scripture you need, in Leviticus 13:40, we're told that "A man who has lost his hair and is bald is clean." Those who suffer from an obviously receding hairline are grafted into the safety of the bald community in the very next verse (Leviticus 13:41).

What I'm trying to say is, bald people are just like you. If you tickle us, do we not laugh? If you prick us, do we not bleed? And if you mock us, do we not send in da bears?

Get Curious

Is there anyone in your life for whom you harbor ill will? What attitude shift will it take for you to long for God's good things even for those who don't treat you kindly?

Failing to Plan

Abraham said of his wife Sarah, "She is my sister."

GENESIS 20:2

Everyone makes mistakes. We see this reflected throughout Scripture, with some of the most glaring examples featuring the fellas. Moses disobeyed God by hitting a rock instead of talking to it (Numbers 20). Peter denied Jesus three times (Mark 14). David stayed home from work, slept with his friend's wife, and then killed his friend to cover it up (2 Samuel 11). Noah got drunk and passed out naked (Genesis 9). The list goes on.

It should come as no surprise, then, that Abraham, the father of many nations, is not immune to mistakes. Some of Abraham's most egregious errors are related to his marital life. Marriage is an important and delicate relationship that should be built on honesty and mutual concern. Abraham obviously didn't get that memo.

> As he was about to enter Egypt, he said to his wife Sarai, "I know what a beautiful woman you are. When the Egyptians see you, they will say, 'This is his wife.' Then they will kill me but will let you live. Say you are my sister, so that I will be treated well for your sake and my life will be spared because of you." (Genesis 12:11–13)

The real shame is that once discovered, Abraham didn't even try to justify the deceit with the obvious "Well, she *is* my sister in Christ" retort.

Relatively speaking, though, not a huge mistake. He didn't have anyone killed, deny ever knowing the Son of God, and his kids didn't see him in his birthday suit. I'm sure he could have eventually gotten past this hiccup. But then he did it again.

> Now Abraham moved on from there into the region of the Negev and lived between Kadesh and Shur. For a while, he stayed in Gerar, and there Abraham said of his wife Sarah, "She is my sister." Then Abimelek king of Gerar sent for Sarah and took her. (Genesis 20:1–2)

It's like Abraham formulated this plan (twice!) and left off at a certain spot. "We'll say you're my sister. That way, they won't kill me if they take you. And if they do end up taking you…Let's just touch base on that over email after lunch."

Both of these stories end with the king returning Sarah to Abraham. I shudder to think what the long chariot ride home must have been like. There was probably very little *shalom* in Abraham's home.

As half-baked as Abraham's plan was, it isn't all that different from our plans. We assess what we can assess, we aspire to what we know to aspire to, but there are always things we miss. Always aspects of our plans that fall short.

God tells the exiled Israelites in Jeremiah 29:11, "I know the plans I have for you." We can take solace knowing that the God of the Bible is a God of wise and holy plans. Ours is not a universe governed by chaos, but by meticulous order.

We may not always see the connections, or the intentions, or even the final destinations, but it is interconnected, intentional, and for our ultimate good.

Most importantly, we can rest in knowing that this cosmic, universal plan was not created by Abraham or Sarah who, in a later problem-solving brainstorm, suggested Abraham hook up with another woman to improve their family situation (Genesis 16:2).

Spoiler alert: It does not.

Get Curious

Is it hard for you to let God do the planning for you? How willing are you to wait rather than do an end run around God's plans?

How We'll Be Remembered

In his old age, however, his feet became diseased.

1 KINGS 15:23

I want my kids to think of me as a good dad, to invite me to their class on career day, and one day deliver a sentimental speech at the opening of the park they donated and named after me.

Because I want my kids to think of me as a good dad, I try to do fun things for them. Things I work hard and spend a lot of money on. We've been to Disney parks several times. Each trip, I spend considerable time working to acquire the perfect "fast passes" so they can ride all their favorite rides and meet all their favorite Star Wars characters.

Also, one time I chased them around the house with a tiny squirt gun. Do you know which of those experiences they talk about the most? I'll give you a hint, it's the one where I was yelling "pew, pew" the whole time. Actually, now that I think about it, that happened in both scenarios. Okay, I'll just tell you, it was the squirt gun.

It's tough to anticipate how people are going to think and what they'll find memorable.

King Asa didn't have much control over how people remembered him. King Asa was, by all accounts, a good king with many good things going for him. "Asa's heart was fully committed to the LORD all his life" (1 Kings 15:14). He tore down idols, waged valiant battles, and even deposed his own grandmother because she was leading people astray (1 Kings 15:13).

And yet, here's one of the last words we get on Asa:

> As for all the other events of Asa's reign, all his achievements, all he did and the cities he built, are they not written in the book of the annals of the kings of Judah? In his old age, however, his feet became diseased. (1 Kings 15:23)

King Asa—king of Judah, builder of cities, and sufferer of foot disease.

The desire to be well-thought-of is pretty second nature to all humans, but ultimately, there is no way we can predict how people will remember us. We should live our lives accordingly.

Many of us do things in an attempt to manipulate a perception over which we have no control. We think if we do *this*, people will think *that* about us. If we take on that extra project at work, they'll think we're extra committed to the cause. If we give to that GoFundMe, they'll think we're generous. If we wear our Tae Kwon Do black belt in public, they'll be intimidated by us (that one's 100 percent true).

King Asa couldn't control how the Bible memorialized him for all eternity any more than you can control what people will think about you. I do know, as Eleanor Roosevelt said so well, "You wouldn't worry so much about what others think of you if you realized how seldom they do." King Asa was a king, like of a whole country, and I bet you haven't thought about him much at all prior to these last couple of minutes.

God has a way before us, full of unique opportunities and challenges. The only thing we can control is our commitment to follow that path, one step at a time. We can't get distracted trying to chase affirmation from others. If we do, we'll just end up with tired, worn-out feet. And honestly, that's all anyone will be talking about.

Get Curious

How much do you value what other people think of you? How often do you do things simply to sway people's opinion of you?

Knock, Knock

*When she recognized Peter's voice, she was
so overjoyed she ran back without opening it
and exclaimed, "Peter is at the door!"
"You're out of your mind," they told her.*

ACTS 12:14–15

I was in a prayer group on New Year's Eve 1999. There were several prayer requests that night: sickness, wisdom, a couple of "unspokens" (which were prayer requests that you presented to the group but you didn't want to talk about), and, oh yeah, that the world wouldn't dissolve into utter chaos when the clock struck midnight. The impending threat of Y2K was definitely the main event of the meeting.

After we submitted our prayer requests, we began the ancient spiritual discipline of popcorn prayer, which is kind of like regular group prayer, but with long, awkward silences mixed in. As we were praying, tensely waiting to see who would pray next, then praying again, midnight came and went.

Our biggest prayer request of the night had been answered with a resounding "everything's fine," and we didn't even notice because we had moved on to praying traveling mercies over Brenda's upcoming trip.

We were so busy praying that we missed that our prayers were answered.

Lest you feel concerned that this is a new problem for the church, I assure you, it's a learned behavior.

In the book of Acts, a group of people got together to pray for Peter, who had been recently thrown into jail. Their prayers were answered when an angel released Peter from jail, but then they almost messed the whole thing up:

> Peter knocked at the outer entrance, and a servant named Rhoda came to answer the door. When she recognized Peter's voice, she was so overjoyed she ran back without opening it and exclaimed, "Peter is at the door!" "You're out of your mind," they told her. (Acts 12:13–15)

"God, please bring Peter home safe."

"Guys! Peter's home safe!"

"Girl, please."

I believe, and I tell others, that God answers prayer, but too often my response to answered prayer tells a different story. I have a good friend named Kim who always says she is "praying expectantly" for things. I make fun of her for it all the time (as she prays expectantly for packages to arrive on time for birthdays). But I envy this character trait of hers, her unwavering trust.

It's a daunting proposition to pray expectantly. To be invested is dangerous. It opens us up to disappointment. To toss out a half-hearted prayer is easy. We get to check a box that says we prayed for it, and if the prayer goes unanswered, we can say "Eh, guess God said no."

There's a great story about Elijah recorded in 1 Kings 18 where he prays for rain, then immediately tells his servant

to go look and see if it's happening yet. It's not, so he prays again. This is the way I want to pray. I want to pray like I believe it means something when I do. I want to pray in a way that I'm not surprised when it happens.

I can, however, relate to a degree of shock when it happens as quickly as it does in this story about Peter. It's the same experience I have when I order something from Amazon and it comes same-day. It's a little odd, it's unexpected, but you've got to keep an eye out for it or someone will steal it off your porch.

Get Curious

Do you pray for big things, things that seem impossible? If you don't, what's stopping you? If you do, do you really believe God can do it?

Forget-Me-Not

He is not here; he has risen!
Remember how he told you.

LUKE 24:6

Telling me the same thing multiple times is condescending, inefficient, and absolutely necessary.

I forget things. Sometimes immediately after I've been told. Have you ever asked someone their name and literally forgotten it as they were telling you?

Sometimes it's not even my fault. My wife, Rachael, sends me to the store for an item, I get in my car, love the song playing on the radio, so I turn it up. I drive by new construction and wonder what they're putting up there. Then I get to a stoplight and I glance down at my odometer to see that I'm about to pass a big milestone number, so I reflect on how much my car and I have been through together. At this point, I literally don't even remember where I was going, let alone what I was supposed to do once I got there. If that song hadn't been so good, none of this would have happened.

Another of my classic moves is to specifically go to a particular store because I have a gift card, shop for whatever I need, then completely forget to pay with the gift card.

Literally, the *one* thing I need to remember at the moment, I forget.

I can definitely relate to the disciples when Jesus was taken and crucified and they were immediately scattered, disoriented, and afraid. It's not their fault. There's no way any of them could have seen this coming. Right?

> From that time on Jesus began to explain to his disciples that he must go to Jerusalem and suffer many things at the hands of the elders, the chief priests and the teachers of the law, and that he must be killed and on the third day be raised to life. (Matthew 16:21)

> He said to them, "The Son of Man is going to be delivered into the hands of men. They will kill him, and after three days he will rise." But they did not understand what he meant and were afraid to ask him about it. (Mark 9:31–32)

> Jesus took the Twelve aside and told them, "We are going up to Jerusalem, and everything that is written by the prophets about the Son of Man will be fulfilled. He will be delivered over to the Gentiles. They will mock him, insult him and spit on him; they will flog him and kill him. On the third day he will rise again." The disciples did not understand any of this. (Luke 18:31–34)

Pretty inconsiderate of Jesus not to give the fellas a heads-up.

I imagine them gathered in a room with a resurrected

Jesus when Andrew finally pipes up and says, "You know what, all this is actually starting to ring a bell."

These were the very people who started the entire Christian movement.

The path Jesus invites us on is a lifelong journey. No one commits to following Christ and just gets steadily holier and holier and holier until they burst like a sanctified piñata full of wordless gospel bracelets, glitter, and "Testamints." It's a pattern of growth and setbacks. Everyone has to learn, and then be reminded, and then be reminded again.

If you're still wrestling with applying fundamental truths years after learning them, you're in good company.

Don't give up. Keep at it. It's a long road. We'd all be a little farther along with it if any of us could remember where we put our keys.

Get Curious

What truths has God taught you?
What physical reminders could you put
in place to remind you of what you've
learned and where you're going?

When You Should Not Try and Try Again

Either he is musing, or he is relieving himself, or he is on a journey, or perhaps he is asleep and must be awakened.

1 KINGS 18:27 ESV

No matter how hard I try to twist open a bottle that's not a twist top, I'll never open it that way. But that doesn't stop me from grabbing a towel or the bottom of my shirt to reassess my grip and try again. The only thing worse than attempting to open a bottle incorrectly is not attempting it with enough gusto, asking for a bottle opener, and being told, "Oh, it's a twist top."

Consider the pickle of a jammed door. You pull on a door and it doesn't budge, so you assume the door is locked, and you knock. Then you hear those dreaded words, "It's open. Just pull." Obviously, you've already attempted to pull, or you wouldn't have come to the conclusion that it was locked. And the "just" in that comment implies the whole fiasco is on you because you didn't pull hard enough in the first place.

It's important to discern when something we're doing needs more "oomph" and when it's time to call it quits. This is a lesson the prophets of Baal had to learn the hard way.

Elijah challenged the prophets of Baal to a contest. They were both to lay an offering on an altar and then call on their respective deities to send down fire and light the offering. The prophets kicked things off with ceremonial dancing and shouting, but nothing happened. (1 Kings 18:26). Elijah couldn't help himself, and jumped in to salt the wound.

> And at noon Elijah mocked them, saying, "Cry aloud, for he is a god. Either he is musing, or he is relieving himself, or he is on a journey, or perhaps he is asleep and must be awakened." (1 Kings 18:27 ESV)

The prophets of Baal, either upset about Elijah's trash talk or taking his advice to heart, cranked the amps to eleven and doubled down:

> So they shouted louder and slashed themselves with swords and spears, as was their custom, until their blood flowed. Midday passed, and they continued their frantic prophesying until the time for the evening sacrifice. But there was no response, no one answered, no one paid attention. (1 Kings 18:28–29)

There's a group of people scream-dancing around a dead animal with swords and spears and no one's even paying attention anymore. That's how sad this scene has gotten.

I find myself in the shoes of the prophets of Baal far too often. Not on the "worshiping a pagan god" front, but on the "maybe if I just try it harder" front. My first instinct when I realize something's not working is to keep trying. Try harder. Try more.

While perseverance is important and a critical element of any successful endeavor, sometimes when we just keep trying, we end up burned out, hurt, and no closer to our goal.

A script-writing professor in college gave this advice: If a story's not working, take one element and turn it upside-down. What if the project they were working on succeeded instead of failed? What if the date went awkwardly instead of perfectly? How would that change the story? Not every question led to a productive plot point, but the act of jostling these key story points around and approaching them differently usually showed the right way to move forward.

There's a fine line between being insane and being insistent. The prophets of Baal are on one side, and a hand that has not been destroyed by a bottle cap is on the other.

Get Curious

Is what you're doing getting the results you want? Is God asking you to be insistent or asking you to shift gears?

THE MARKET VALUE OF MANDRAKES

"Very well," Rachel said, "he can sleep with you tonight in return for your son's mandrakes."

GENESIS 30:15

I f movies featuring melodramatic businessmen have taught me anything, it's that everything in this world has a price. Everything has a number. A monetary value. My wife set a price on my head a few years ago.

We were expecting our first child, so we decided to sign up for life insurance—you know, in case I get trapped in a coal mine collapse and my helpless wife and child are left to fend for themselves. (My office job made this scenario unlikely, although not altogether impossible, hence the insurance.) My wife made the initial call and handled all the detailed questions about my height, weight, birthday, etc. Then the lady from the insurance company asked her a pretty simple question:

"What would you say your husband is worth?"

Rachael replied that she didn't understand the question. The insurance lady told her to guesstimate a number reflecting how much, monetarily, she thought I was worth. My wife said she still wasn't sure how to answer. Then, "to make things simple," the lady suggested that my wife just put that I'm worth $0.

And my wife agreed.

Gumballs carry a higher suggested retail value than I do. I'm not worth a stamp. If you pulled up to a gas station with two of me in your pocket, you couldn't put air in your tires.

That is, in the eyes of my wife.

Obviously, this is my story with just one wife. But Jacob has two wives and receives a different assessment:

> Rachel said to Leah, "Please give me some of your son's mandrakes." But she said to her, "Wasn't it enough that you took away my husband? Will you take my son's mandrakes too?" "Very well," Rachel said, "he can sleep with you tonight in return for your son's mandrakes." So when Jacob came in from the fields that evening, Leah went out to meet him. "You must sleep with me," she said. "I have hired you with my son's mandrakes." So he slept with her that night. (Genesis 30:14–16)

Jacob's wife, Rachel, sells him to his other wife, Leah, for some mandrakes. Are you familiar with mandrakes? They're like carrots, but uglier.

There's real danger in basing our worth on the opinion of others. If my self-image is based on what other people think about me, then I subject myself to the natural ebbs and flows of whatever is going on in *their* life. A good friend having a bad day can become *my* identity crisis. It's unfair to me, to them, and to the mandrakes who are unwitting pawns in this whole game.

Even the people who love us most in this world will have moments when they'd sell us down the river for a bushel of misshapen carrots.

If you ever question your worth, pause for a moment and contemplate how much God loves you. God loves you constantly, consistently, selflessly, unconditionally. A right understanding of this is critical to a balanced sense of self.

Jacob's wives assess him at a higher value than I was assessed. This is simply an example of the economic principle called supply and demand. I have one wife and she gets me all the time. The demand for me is low. Jacob has two wives and they have to split time with him. So demand is... also pretty low, as it turns out. But at least mandrakes are something.

Get Curious

What is your primary source of self-worth? Is it from your relationships, your accomplishments, your abilities, your reputation, or from God's view of you?

circumstantial circumstances

They had difficulty keeping the crowd from sacrificing to them. Then some Jews came from Antioch and Iconium and won the crowd over. They stoned Paul and dragged him outside the city.

ACTS 14:18–19

While my wife and I were still dating, her dad asked me to remove a few palm trees from his backyard. Desperate to impress him and with zero landscaping experience, I confidently responded, "No problem." Armed with a borrowed shovel, a borrowed pair of gloves, and a can-do attitude, I set out on my task.

I learned pretty quickly that I had bitten off more than I could chew. But still, I toiled away in the Florida summer heat. My future mother-in-law invited me inside for lemonade several times, but I refused. I intended to impress them, and impressive dudes don't stop for lemonade.

Two palm trees down, I finally decided lemonade might not be the worst idea.

I went inside and sat down. The whole family seemed in awe of my fortitude. They didn't say it out loud. In fact, it looked as if they were all just going about their day. But deep down it was clear that they were impressed. That is until I ran into the bathroom and threw up everywhere.

Evidently fortitude only goes so far.

Suddenly, my future in-laws' silent admiration of my mettle turned into not-so-silent displeasure of my mess.

In an instant, the whole situation flipped.

Barnabas and Paul knew something about that. One minute they were being praised as gods:

> Barnabas they called Zeus, and Paul they called Hermes because he was the chief speaker. (Acts 14:12)

> Even with these words, they had difficulty keeping the crowd from sacrificing to them. (Acts 14:18)

Literally one verse later, they stoned Paul and left him for dead:

> Then some Jews came from Antioch and Iconium and won the crowd over. They stoned Paul and dragged him outside the city, thinking he was dead. (Acts 14:19)

I don't know what Paul threw up on to deserve this change of fortunes, but it must have been very expensive.

Our circumstances are constantly changing. Finances, reputations, jobs, relationships, culture, health—none of it is certain. I think this is why Scripture talks so much about steadfastness, endurance, and faithfulness. If we can only do something when circumstances are ideal, we will not accomplish much. If our progress depends on convenience, then our progress will come very slowly, if at all.

Staying disciplined is perhaps more difficult today than ever. There is so much to distract us. So many other things to do. When our eyes drift from the path God has set before us, we'll find plenty vying for our attention.

We need to stay focused on the person God is calling us to be and the path God has set before us. Our circumstances are ever-changing, mostly beyond our control, and ultimately a distraction.

When we focus on the task at hand, we're better equipped to handle the things we can control (like staying hydrated, for example). When we focus on impressing people (something we can't control), we're far more likely to hurl on the vanity in the master bath.

Get Curious

What potential stressors are outside of your control? What self-care tasks can you accomplish every day? (Examples: Drink plenty of water, read your Bible, spend time in prayer, take the stairs, take a walk, do deep breathing exercises, etc.)

EXCUSES, EXCUSES

*So I told them, "Whoever has any
gold jewelry, take it off." Then they gave me
the gold, and I threw it into the fire,
and out came this calf!*

EXODUS 32:24

When I was little, I always left my backpack at school. To be fair, I didn't focus solely on forgetting my backpack. My thermos, my sweatshirts, my shoes, really anything that came with me to school was likely to be, as my friend Kirk Cameron would say, "Left Behind."

Another quick note about me when I was little—I used to lie. A lot. Big lies, too. Like the time I told my teacher that my aunt and uncle were missionaries in Papua New Guinea. (I was found out when my teacher called and asked my mom if we had any pictures that she could show the class.)

Or the time I told all my friends that for my birthday party, we were going to drive to Orlando in a double-decker bus/ limo where my uncle (who worked for the NBA) was going to get us tickets to the Magic vs. Bulls game. (Which ended up being just a birthday party at my house because my "uncle" was "fired" from his "job.")

One day I came home without my backpack (again), and my mom and stepdad decided this was the last straw. How embarrassing for them when I informed them the janitor (or teacher or principal, I honestly don't remember) *stole* my backpack and that's why I didn't have it.

My parents asked me to clarify more about the story (I can only assume so they could alert the appropriate authorities about the janitorial heist), and my story began to fall apart. Much to everyone's surprise, I had made the whole thing up.

Biblically speaking, in the Old Testament, Aaron found himself in a similar situation. And while my excuse was flimsy at best, his borders on miraculous. Moses gets back from receiving the Ten Commandments to find the Israelites worshiping a golden calf. He asks Aaron what happened, and this is how Aaron responds:

> They said to me, "Make us gods who will go before us..." So I told them, "Whoever has any gold jewelry, take it off." Then they gave me the gold, and I threw it into the fire, and out came this calf! (Exodus 32:23–24)

Obviously mistake number one here is that he assisted the Israelites in creating an idol to worship instead of being patient and waiting on God. But a close second is this travesty of an excuse as to why he did it.

(At least find a way to work in an out-of-town uncle. C'mon, Aaron.)

Sometimes our lies don't seem so outrageous.

"I'm only gonna eat one of your fries."

"We're just friends."

"I'm on my way."

The crazy thing is, these lies might even fool some people, people who don't know us very well. But our true friends, the people closest to us, know better. They knew you were still in bed when you sent that last one as a text.

This is the way God feels about you. God sees you, knows you, and still wants to hang out with you.

The relationship between people and God has been full of lies and excuses since the very beginning. Our excuses are as uninteresting to God now as they were then.

God knows you made the calf, and God still wants you to be a leader.

God knows how many fries you're going to take, and God still wants to share.

God knows you're running late, but God still wants you to come to the party.

Get Curious

What lie—large or small—or what excuse do you need to "come clean" about with God? Knowing you are seen, known, and unconditionally loved, what's the risk?

The Worst

With such nagging she prodded him day after day until he was sick to death of it.

JUDGES 16:16

Honesty is the best policy, but not always an easy one. Like when kids two and under get into Disney free and you're there the day after your kid's third birthday.

Few have known the tension of wanting to be honest yet seeing the obvious benefits of being dishonest better than Samson.

> Delilah said to Samson, "Tell me the secret of your great strength and how you can be tied up and subdued." (Judges 16:6)

At least a little suspicion had to arise with this oddly specific question. Obviously, Samson was concerned, because he gave her a fake answer:

> Samson answered her, "If anyone ties me with seven fresh bowstrings that have not been dried, I'll become as weak as any other man." (Judges 16:7)

Shortly after this, in the strangest of "coincidences," Samson was ambushed and tied up with seven fresh bowstrings by his archrivals, the Philistines. Bowstrings, how-ever, were not the secret of his strength, so Samson bested his enemies and fought himself free.

One would assume Delilah would be sheepish about her plot having been exposed. One would be wrong.

> Then Delilah said to Samson, "You have made a fool of me; you lied to me. Come now, tell me how you can be tied." (Judges 16:10)

I would say "making a fool of" would fall just under "conspiracy to commit murder" as far as the severity of of-fenses goes.

The crazy "coincidences" continue with "new ropes" and "putting a weave in his hair." (I may not be understand-ing that last one totally right.)

Until finally this:

> Then she said to him, "How can you say, 'I love you,' when you won't confide in me?…" With such nagging she prodded him day after day until he was sick to death of it. So he told her everything. (Judges 16:15–17)

Samson told Delilah that his hair was the secret to his strength and, in a twist as shocking as my uncle's thumb ac-tually not disconnecting from his hand during his magic trick, these were, in fact, not coincidences. Delilah was conspir-ing to help the Philistines capture Samson the whole time. Delilah put Samson in a position where, after surveying his options, lying made the most sense.

Some people have this effect on us. They put us in compromising situations where the best decision is a bad one. Other people encourage us to be the best version of ourselves. They challenge us, push us, and celebrate with us when we experience growth. These are the people we want to go to for hair-cutting advice.

If you want to be more honest, surround yourself with honest people. If you want to be more generous, surround yourself with generous people. We should choose the relationships that propel us into the best version of the person God made us to be, and avoid those who force us to choose between two versions we don't like.

And never, under any circumstances, should we let someone pressure us into getting a haircut. Everyone's always "get a perm," "cut it short," "shave it off." But you know what? It's not their hair. It's your hair. They don't have to live with the consequences.

Take it from me, Samson, and Rapunzel. You never really appreciate your hair until it's gone.

Get Curious

Who do you spend the most time with?
What do you admire about them?
Does their company make you more like
the person you'd like to be?

What Happens When We Assume

When Haman entered, the king asked him, "What should be done for the man the king delights to honor?" Now Haman thought to himself, "Who is there that the king would rather honor than me?"

ESTHER 6:6

Bad things happen when we make assumptions. There is perhaps no greater or more poignant cautionary tale about assumption than the story of Haman.

Haman is a painfully insecure villain who gets promoted to a really powerful position by King Xerxes. King Xerxes gives Haman a "seat of honor higher than that of all the other nobles" (Esther 3:1). That only turns out to augment his insecurities. So much so that he spends his days perpetually bothered by one normal guy, Mordecai, who refuses to bow down to him when he walks past (Esther 3:2).

The only thing that seems to bring Haman any sense of consolation when dealing with this constant snubbing is his plan to one day exact revenge on his disrespectful nemesis.

His wife Zeresh and all his friends said to him, "Have a pole set up...and ask the king in the morning to have

Mordecai impaled on it…" This suggestion delighted Haman. (Esther 5:14)

Haman's wife seems sweet.

The story continues when Haman shows up for work one day and King Xerxes greets him with a question.

The king asked him, "What should be done for the man the king delights to honor?" Now Haman thought to himself, "Who is there that the king would rather honor than me?" (Esther 6:6)

Haman assumes he's the one the king's referring to, and who could blame him? With all those impaling plans he's been drawing up, it's about time someone took notice of his hard work. Since he believes he's the one receiving the honor, Haman gives a very specific suggestion involving special robes, a parade, and a personal escort/town crier (Esther 6:8–9).

Haman has clearly been waiting for the king to ask him this question for months (there's no other way you could have that kind of detail prepared). So imagine how excited Haman must have been when the king was hyped on his idea.

"Go at once," the king commanded Haman. "Get the robe and the horse and do just as you have suggested…" (Esther 6:10)

And how devastated he was about this twist:

"…for Mordecai." (Esther 6:10)

And how enthusiastic he probably was while doing this:

So Haman got the robe and the horse. He robed Mordecai, and led him on horseback through the city streets, proclaiming before him, "This is what is done for the man the king delights to honor!" (Esther 6:11)

Irony hits hard and, as it turns out, it was just getting warmed up.

They impaled Haman on the pole he had set up for Mordecai. (Esther 7:10)

Assumptions can be dangerous, for some more literally than others. I make assumptions all the time. I assume someone is disinterested because they don't immediately respond to my text. I assume someone is mad at me because of a short exchange we shared when we ran into each other at Target. I assume someone is having a bad day because they are quietly minding their own business and something is obviously wrong with me.

Assumptions may be hazardous, but they are also easily avoided. Usually it requires little more than a timely and honest question. *When you say that, do you mean...? Did you hear me when I said...? I heard about what happened. Are you feeling...? Is this reward for me? Because, if so, I have ideas...*

We can all learn from the mistakes of Haman and others. We need to take time to clarify assumptions. We'll avoid a lot of uncomfortable situations if we do.

Get Curious

Are you operating on an assumption
right now? What would it hurt to ask
a quick clarifying question?

Bully for You

Ish-Bosheth did not dare to say another word
to Abner, because he was afraid of him.

2 SAMUEL 3:11

As commander of Saul's army, Abner was one of the first "bullies" in recorded history. He wasn't a cyberbully, hiding behind anonymous comments and burner Twitter accounts. Abner was a classic archetype, a Biff from *Back to the Future* kind of bully.

Although the term had not been popularized yet, you can see in Abner all the traits common in the classic bully.

He traveled with a posse:

When Abner, who had twenty men with him, came to David at Hebron, David prepared a feast for him and his men. (2 Samuel 3:20)

He was regularly uninformed:

As Saul watched David going out to meet the Philistine, he said to Abner, commander of the army, "Abner, whose son is that young man?" Abner replied, "...I don't know." (1 Samuel 17:55)

He liked watching people get hurt:

Then Abner said to Joab, "Let's have some of the young men get up and fight hand to hand in front of us." (2 Samuel 2:14)

He intimidated people:

Then Abner said to him, "Go back home!" So he
   went back. (2 Samuel 3:16)
Abner conferred with the elders of Israel and said,
   "For some time you have wanted to make David
   your king. Now do it!" (2 Samuel 3:17–18)
Ish-Bosheth did not dare to say another word to Abner,
   because he was afraid of him. (2 Samuel 3:11)

He was violent:

Abner thrust the butt of his spear into Asahel's
stomach, and the spear came out through his back.
(2 Samuel 2:23)

Abner was an "enforcer" of sorts for King Saul through-out the king's conflict with David. He was the commander of Saul's army and a deadly antagonist in David's story. But in a surprise twist, Abner eventually came to David, wanting to help facilitate peace and reunite Israel. Abner does not get to see this peace, however, as Joab (commander of David's army) kills him shortly after it's initiated.

As a longtime enemy of David, it would certainly seem understandable for David not to feel this loss too greatly. Sure, Abner seems to have had a dramatic change of heart at the end of the story (alarmingly on-brand for a bully), but it definitely could be interpreted to most as a mere glimmer of "good" after years of "bad."

David's response was quite the opposite. He called down a curse on Joab for his actions, led his country into a time of mourning for their enemy, and wept aloud as they laid Abner to rest (2 Samuel 3:29–32). After everything he'd done, David still saw Abner as his brother.

It's hard to get your head around this kind of treatment for Biff, but it's a beautiful application of the world-changing truth God intends us to learn. Everyone we see, everyone we interact with—no matter where they come from or what they've done—are in a sense, family. They are sisters. They are brothers.

From close friends to the Biffs of the world, we're all human beings created by God. It's the image of God we bear, the breath of God in our lungs. Ultimately, what we have in common far outweighs anything that would otherwise pull us apart.

Get Curious

What type of people are the hardest for you to have compassion for? What makes them seem unworthy of compassion? How do you think God views those people?

It's All in the Timing

He went up to it but found nothing on it except leaves. Then he said to it, "May you never bear fruit again!" Immediately the tree withered.

MATTHEW 21:19

There is a time and a place for everything. Except for pizza. That's an any time, any place kind of deal. Timing is everything, they say. Which, I assume, is why I have a whole belt committed to timing in my car.

The Bible shows us the dramatic impact timing can have. Jesus was hungry and spotted a fig tree, but it was not the time of year that fig trees produce their fruit. Which was unfortunate for Jesus…and the tree.

> He went up to it but found nothing on it except leaves. Then he said to it, "May you never bear fruit again!" Immediately the tree withered. (Matthew 21:19)

The first time David met Abigail, the timing was not great. Abigail's husband, Nabal, had slighted and disrespected David, so David was on his way to exact revenge. Abigail intervened, David was assuaged by her, and the two went their separate ways. Nabal died suddenly a few days later, and so the timing changed radically, a fact not lost on David.

When David heard that Nabal was dead, he said, "Praise be to the LORD…" Then David sent word to Abigail, asking her to become his wife. (1 Samuel 25:39)

The book of Ecclesiastes explicitly spells out different "times" or seasons we can expect to experience throughout our lives.

A time to be born and a time to die, a time to plant and a time to uproot. (Ecclesiastes 3:2)

There is a time to get inspired and plant some interesting plants in your garden, and there is a time to accept that they are not "coming back" and are actually brown and dried and sad looking because they're dead.

A time to scatter stones and a time to gather them. (Ecclesiastes 3:5)

There is a time to gather small stones together as a cool landscaping feature, and a time for a child to inevitably take those stones and scatter them all over the yard.

A time to embrace and a time to refrain from embracing. (Ecclesiastes 3:5)

There is a time to hug Aunt Nancy at Thanksgiving and a time to cut her off from her cider and her hugs when she's going in for fourths and fifths.

A time to search and a time to give up.
(Ecclesiastes 3:6)

There is a time to keep humming the chorus as you try to find the song that's stuck in your head, and there's a time to realize "something something something my heart something" is not a Google search that will get you where you want to go.

A time to keep and a time to throw away.
(Ecclesiastes 3:6)

There is a tiny hole in your favorite socks that's probably fine, and then there's a completely exposed heel that says it may be time to part ways.

Whether good or bad, whatever time we're in, it is only for a time.

So, we hold on to hope relentlessly. We are a people of hope. Hope that things can and will get better. Hope that love can and will win in the end.

Hope that this next plant in the garden will be the one that makes it (he said, as he brought home his fourth fiddle-leaf fig).

Get curious

Are you in a good moment? How can you
soak it up? Are you in a tough moment?
How can you get through today and
maintain hope for tomorrow?

What's in a Name?

Pharaoh gave Joseph the name Zaphenath-Paneah.

GENESIS 41:45

My birth certificate may say my name is Anthony, but I don't get called that a lot. My given name is just a jumping-off point for people. Here are a few of the monikers I have answered to over the years:

Ant'ny
Antonio
Antwan
Anth
Ant
Ant-Man
Tony
Tony the Tiger
Tone
T-Bone
Tone Balogn
Stinky

I'd rather not talk about that last one.

I've never had a real strong preference for what people called me, which would have made me well equipped for Bible times because names were changing left and right.

(Moses gave Hoshea son of Nun the name Joshua.)
(Numbers 13:16)

Moses really did us all a favor by making this switcheroo. "Hoshea fought the battle of Jericho" just doesn't have the same ring to it.

Pharaoh gave Joseph the name Zaphenath-Paneah. (Genesis 41:45)

It's concerning how much Joseph's new name sounds like my mom's attempt at saying, "Zach Galifianakis."

She gave birth to a son, and they named him Solomon. The Lord loved him; and because the Lord loved him, he sent word through Nathan the prophet to name him Jedidiah. (2 Samuel 12:24–25)

Have you ever met someone who goes by "Chris" but their first name's "Bartholomew"? That's what I imagine happened here. David and Bathsheba can't rightly disagree with God in the naming of a child, so Solomon probably moves over to middle name status, and yet very few people call it "Jedidiah's Temple."

No longer will you be called Abram; your name will be Abraham. (Genesis 17:5)

This had to turn into one of those situations where your name is actually Kirstin but everyone calls you Kristin and it ends up being an everyday struggle.

As for Sarai your wife, you are no longer to call her
Sarai; her name will be Sarah. (Genesis 17:15)

Sarah is a classic name that has stood the test of time.
Sarai has that millennial, celebrity baby name vibe. I can't be
sure, but I would guess that's why God changed it.

Your name will no longer be Jacob, but Israel.
(Genesis 32:28)

People don't even realize when they say the word
"Israel" they're saying a person's name. While most people
still tell his stories using the name "Jacob," facts are facts.
This guy's name is Israel and he has his own flag.

Jesus looked at him and said, "You are Simon son
of John. You will be called Cephas" (which, when
translated, is Peter). (John 1:42)

Cephas (and its more common Greek translation—Peter)
both mean Rock. Simon goes from sharing a name with the
guy who "says" to sharing a name with a wrestler/action
movie star/national treasure. It's a real "rags to riches" story
on several levels.

As important as names are today, they were even more
defining to a person in biblical context. Jesus changes
Simon's name to Peter because Jesus sees him. He knows
who he is, who he was, and who he is going to be. The only
one who can correctly name you is the one who can correctly
see you.

It's comforting to know that nothing has the final word

on defining us. Successes, failures, culture, friends, family, and strangers on the internet may explicitly or implicitly try to define us, but ultimately, they will not and cannot.

God sees you. God knows you. God loves you. God names you (see Isaiah 62:2 and Revelation 2:17).

And God would never call you Stinky.

Get Curious

How do you think people in your life view you? How do you see yourself? How does it change daily life and your thoughts about the future to know how God sees you?

Bull Stuff

If, however, the bull has had the habit
of goring...

EXODUS 21:29

I try to keep an ongoing tally of danger vs. benefit, risk vs. reward.

For example, when I need to get on my roof, I use my old ladder. It's got the faintest little wobble (not enough to actually be hazardous, but enough to sporadically make my stomach drop) and it's not much to look at, but by using it, I both safely get on my roof and put off the expenditure of a new ladder. While the ladder may be a little suspect, the benefits supersede the danger.

Alternatively, I live in Florida, so my power bill is very high, particularly in the summer. Windmills are an alternative source of energy. If I installed a windmill in my backyard, I would probably spend less on power every month. But think about all that valuable time I would lose trying to putt-putt a golf ball through it. The downside of the windmill supersedes the benefit.

In the second book of the Bible, we come across the better part of a chapter full of policies that start like this:

If a bull gores a man or woman... (Exodus 21:28)
...if the bull gores a son or daughter... (Exodus 21:31)

If anyone's bull injures someone else's bull…
   (Exodus 21:35)
If, however, the bull has had the habit of goring…
   (Exodus 21:29)

I'm sure bulls were useful to the ancient Israelites. But this degree of contingency planning makes me question if the bulls are worth the risk. Maybe it's time to consider getting rid of the bulls. Or, at the very least, limiting bulls. Or collectively stop wearing red. (But then, how would we know who works at Target?)

The danger/benefit metric is a good one to remember when assessing lots of things in life. A habit, a relationship, or a tradition may actually cause more harm than good. Boundaries and contingency plans are helpful. But sometimes we need to consider if it's time for it to go.

That course of action may feel extreme, but the Bible gives precedent in a couple of ways. If it's a destructive habit, look to Jesus' teaching. He said when your right hand causes you to sin, you should part ways with it (Matthew 5:30). That might seem extreme, but His point was that no matter how valuable it is to you, if it's causing sin/harm, it's not worth it.

If you need to create distance from a destructive person, look to Paul. Paul was not hesitant to create distance in toxic relationships and even did it publicly with both Demas (2 Timothy 4:10) and Alexander the blacksmith (2 Timothy 4:14).

In my life, I have encountered more gray issues than black-and-white ones. There is so much freedom in our relationship with Christ. But as Paul so perfectly articulated in 1 Corinthians, "'I have the right to do anything'—but not

everything is constructive" (10:23). If you're looking to defend your right to keep something in your life, you probably have it. But you should be slow to defend those rights, and much quicker to identify what is constructive and what is not.

Bulls may be very strong, and enticing to run with, and fun to grab by the horns, but they are an absolute menace to china shop owners. And, honestly, I think we should all be doing our best to support the china shop owners in our community.

Get Curious

Is there anything in your life that you find yourself regularly defending? What are the positive elements or benefits it brings? What are the negative? Is it worth it?

A Dash of Disappointment

So the three mighty warriors broke through the Philistine lines, drew water from the well near the gate of Bethlehem, and carried it back to David. But he refused to drink it.

2 SAMUEL 23:16

One Valentine's Day, I thought it would be romantic if I made Rachael dinner. So I Googled "best dish to make for Valentine's Day." The internet, in its infinite wisdom, recommended I make strawberry chicken. Strawberries seemed pretty Valentinesey, so the suggestion made sense to me.

My wife (girlfriend at the time) watched a lot of Food Network, so I could only imagine how impressed she was going to be by my grand gesture. I thought about her describing the dish like a judge on *Iron Chef*. Stuff like, "This chicken is seasoned perfectly," or "The strawberries really tie the whole dish together," or "You're so handsome and funny, let's make out." A boy can dream.

The dish seemed simple enough, and I knew my way around a kitchen (by that I mean I was a part-time busboy at Red Lobster), so I finalized my plan.

I unveiled my great plan to Rachael later that day, which is also when I discovered she doesn't like strawberries. I was crushed. My chances of winning *Iron Chef*? Destroyed.

My trust in the internet? Devastated. My makeout plans? Dashed.

We went out to eat that night, and eventually got married and had two beautiful kids, a dog, and three hermit crabs, so I guess everything worked out okay, despite the disappointment from my romantic culinary plan backfiring.

Consider the best-laid plans of David's mighty warriors in this story from 2 Samuel:

> David longed for water and said, "Oh, that someone would get me a drink of water from the well near the gate of Bethlehem!" So the three mighty warriors broke through the Philistine lines, drew water from the well near the gate of Bethlehem, and carried it back to David. (2 Samuel 23:15–16)

Like cooking for a rabid Food Network watcher, this surprise seems like a surefire win, doesn't it? David's going to be so pumped to get this water, it will probably result in a three-way tie for "Mighty Warrior of the Month."

> But he refused to drink it; instead, he poured it out before the LORD. "Far be it from me, LORD, to do this!" he said. "Is it not the blood of men who went at the risk of their lives?" And David would not drink it. (2 Samuel 23:16–17)

Like a persnickety coffee drinker presented with a foamy latté, he wouldn't even take a sip.

Sometimes we extend extra effort in a relationship and we don't get the acknowledgment or appreciation we expect. As much as we work and plan, we can't control how people are going to respond. But doing the right thing and going out on a limb for people we love will always have a positive impact on us.

The little things we do to demonstrate our love, the extra time we take—it all matters. It's making us better people and making the world a better place. We can't let one person's minimal or absent response cause us to lose sight of that.

Additional life lesson. It might be a good idea to get a better sense of food preferences before you go diving into a surprise dinner.

Get Curious

When was the last time you were disappointed by someone's response to something you did or said? Was it still worth doing?

No Good Options

*Ahithophel has advised Absalom and the elders
of Israel to do such and such, but I have
advised them to do so and so.*

2 SAMUEL 17:15

After the births of our kids, my wife and I didn't get out much. We mostly changed diapers, made up songs with our newborn's name in them, and never sat down. (How does a completely asleep baby always know when you sit down?)

One day, my in-laws offered to babysit so we could go on a date. This was the first opportunity we'd had in months, so we talked extensively about what we should do. Should we go out to eat? Go for a stroll in the park? Take a nap?

We decided to see a movie. We were thrilled to get the chance to finally enjoy the cinema again (and sit down for two hours). Brimming with anticipation, we checked to see what was showing at our theater. The selection was bleak. I had higher hopes for options on my first kid-free movie outing than *Daddy's Home 2* or *Boo 2! A Madea Halloween*.

Decision making is tough when you're presented with less-than-stellar options. Absalom experienced this in the form of direction from his advisors.

> Hushai told Zadok and Abiathar, the priests,
> "Ahithophel has advised Absalom and the elders of

Israel to do such and such, but I have advised them to do so and so." (2 Samuel 17:15)

Both options are ripe with possibilities. Initially, I lean more toward such and such than so and so, but you know me. I'm kind of an adrenaline junkie.

You can read an unpacking of "such and such" (2 Samuel 17:1–3) and "so and so" (2 Samuel 17:7–13) earlier in the chapter, but the summary is that both pieces of advice suggested pursuing and attacking David (Absalom's father and predecessor as king).

Very few people ever attacked David and his men successfully. I'm not certain the attack strategy was going to play out well whichever way Absalom sliced it.

It's a familiar situation to find yourself having to choose between two limited or two extreme options. I learned recently that these are called "false dichotomies." Identifying and naming false dichotomies has been liberating as I work through problems and make decisions. Let's take an example we all know and care deeply about: pizza.

It used to be that someone would ask what you'd like on your pizza and it was not a particularly defining moment for you as a human being. Maybe you liked pepperoni. Or peppers. Or pineapple. I lost you there, didn't I? Nobody "maybe" likes pineapple on their pizza anymore. Pineapple is either your favorite pizza topping or you think pineapple pizza is a domino in the eventual toppling of Western civilization as we know it.

The world we live in seems to leave less and less room for "I'm not quite sure how I feel about that" or "I'd like to read up a little bit before I commit either way."

When pressed to choose between extreme opinions or forced to pick between limited choices, remember that "such and such" and "so and so" are not the only ways. We have other options. Paths others have walked and completely new trails to blaze.

You may like your pizza in such and such way and your friend may prefer pizza so and so. The deeper truth is that we are all blessed to have pizza in our lives, and it is irrefutable evidence that God loves us.

Get Curious

Which of your opinions do you feel strongest about? What opinions do you hold that may have been born out of false dichotomies?

RUDE

*Then the disciples came to him and asked,
"Do you know that the Pharisees were
offended when they heard this?"*

MATTHEW 15:12

How wude!" I only had to hear this statement from little Michelle Tanner on the original TV show *Full House* one time to know rude was something I didn't want to be. Rude is an overriding characteristic. It doesn't matter what else you are, if you're also rude, it negates the rest.

"I don't want to be rude" is a line of logic that changes my behavior, even when trying to be helpful. I don't want to tell him that plug doesn't go into that slot. I don't want to tell her she has pizza sauce on her shirt. I don't want to tell him Andrew's actually not my name (true story, the guy called me Andrew for a year)...because I don't want to be rude.

My wife and her family are Canadian so, obviously, they get it.

The original disciples of Jesus shared our aversion to rudeness. Jesus had a frequently contentious relationship with the Pharisees. The presence and message of Jesus were unsettling to the established religion of the day, and the Pharisees were the established religion of the day.

In other words, Jesus and his crew were the Jets and the Pharisees and their crew were the Sharks. (At least, I think that's how that goes. I'm not totally sure. I don't watch a ton of hockey.)

One day the Pharisees were picking on Jesus' squad because of some questionable hygiene practices.

> Then some Pharisees and teachers of the law came to Jesus from Jerusalem and asked, "Why do your disciples break the tradition of the elders? They don't wash their hands before they eat!" (Matthew 15:1–2)

Jesus takes up for his boys with (among other things) this retort: You hypocrites! (Matthew 15:7)

Jesus defended the squad. He refused to back down. He stood up for his friends. The disciples...took a different approach to the altercation:

> Then the disciples came to him (Jesus) and asked, "Do you know that the Pharisees were offended when they heard this?" (Matthew 15:12)

What? Yes! Of course, He knows they were offended. He just called them hypocrites. C'mon, guys.

Jesus is out there startin' fights for you, and you're worried about what the other team thinks?

You gotta get off the bench and get in the game. (Full disclosure, I'm not sure if they call it a bench. Or a game. Match, maybe? Like I said, I don't know much about hockey. I do know they only play three quarters which seems wrong, economically speaking.)

The message of Jesus has been, from the beginning, off-putting to some people. The offended are often people in powerful positions with something to lose by a leveled spiritual playing field of equally important image-bearers of God. No one is immune to the offensive impact the gospel can have on human-constructed systems.

The implication to me and you is that truly following the path of Jesus means embracing the possibility that it will be offensive to some. The goal has to change from not offending to willingly offending the societal structures, customs, and positions of power that stand against loving God and loving our neighbors as ourselves.

If someone is offended by your extending grace, empowering others, defending the helpless, affirming others, encouraging others, or inviting someone to the table, offend away.

It would be wude not to.

Get Curious

Do you ever feel hesitant to speak openly about what you believe? What is it you think the hearer would find offensive? Are you willing to risk offending for what you believe?

Bought-In or Kicked-Out

The LORD said to Gideon, "You have too many
men. I cannot deliver Midian into their hands."

JUDGES 7:2

"The more the merrier" is not so much a saying as a lifestyle for me. I want everyone to be involved, everyone invited. I would have had five thousand people at my wedding if chair rentals weren't so expensive. If I receive a Facebook friend request with no mutual friends listed and no inkling as to how I know this person, everything in me still wants to accept.

So, naturally, it pains me to read the story of Gideon. Gideon is leading the people of God against the oppressive Midianites. He's camped out with his forces when he receives this word from God:

> The LORD said to Gideon, "You have too many men. I cannot deliver Midian into their hands, or Israel would boast against me, 'My own strength has saved me.'" (Judges 7:2)

Gideon must have been confused. (It's been a while since I read *The Art of War*, but I'm fairly sure "have a big army" is one of the suggestions.) But who doesn't love an underdog story, right?

> Now announce to the army, "Anyone who trembles
> with fear may turn back and leave Mount Gilead." So,
> twenty-two thousand men left, while ten thousand
> remained. (Judges 7:3)

So Gideon is left with ten thousand liars. *Everyone* was probably scared. Maybe it's good to expel outspoken fear out of the camp. They were bringing bad energy anyway. The last dismissal, however, is a little more difficult to wrap my mind around.

> So Gideon took the men down to the water. There
> the LORD told him, "Separate those who lap the water
> with their tongues as a dog laps from those who kneel
> down to drink." Three hundred of them drank from
> cupped hands, lapping like dogs. (Judges 7:5–6)

After removing the scaredy cats, and identifying the dog drinkers, Gideon's army dwindles from thirty-two thousand to three hundred.

If you're anything like me (and probably Gideon), you feel better when you have people—a posse, tribe, crew—around you, supporting you, cheering you on, maybe even accomplishing the task with you.

While the story of Gideon reducing his squad makes me cringe every time I read it, the rationale God teaches is important. Do you ever find yourself under-resourced for the challenge in front of you?

I've never met a parent who feels they have enough energy or parental wisdom to raise their kids. Or an entrepreneur who says they have enough resources to make their

company work. Or an artist who has enough time to create. These are all familiar stories. What is remarkable is that they look the deficit in the eyes and press forward anyway.

The story of Gideon and his dog-lapping soldiers reminds us that we have always had enough. God is with us, God is for us, and because of that we *are* enough.

Romans 8:31 says it this way: "If God is for us, who can be against us?" Wherever we are, whatever's in front of us, we have what we need. People in our life will come and go. Some will be life-giving, helpful, and supportive. Others will drink water the wrong way, and we'll have to send them home.

Regardless of how many people are on your side, if you're following after God, I like your odds.

Get Curious

Do you feel like you have the resources to do what God is calling you to do? What's stopping you from starting where you are and moving forward with what you have?

Red Light

Remnant of Judah, the LORD has told you,
"Do not go to Egypt."
JEREMIAH 42:19

You know that conversation you have with your friend? The one where she says, "...so he doesn't technically have a 'job' but he's thinking about doing some freelance life coaching"?

Then she says she really wants your advice about moving forward with a relationship because she trusts you. So you remind her of her last relationship with a guy like this, tactfully bring up how poorly that ended, beg her to reconsider, and a few weeks later you see pictures on Instagram of the two of them in an escape room.

Jeremiah was like you. The Israelites were like your friend.

The remnant of Israel (all the people left over after Babylon came and snatched the majority of Israel away) approaches Jeremiah to say, "Hey, it seems like we may have made a mistake in not listening to God. As it happens, we are now an utterly destroyed and maligned people; and we feel like we are ready to listen to God's instructions."

Jeremiah speaks with God on behalf of Israel, and the word he returns with has a pretty strong central theme.

> If you stay in this land, I will build you up and not tear
> you down. (Jeremiah 42:10)
> If you are determined to go to Egypt and you do
> go to settle there, then the sword you fear will
> overtake you there, and the famine you dread
> will follow you into Egypt, and there you will die.
> (Jeremiah 42:15–16)
> As my anger and wrath have been poured out on
> those who lived in Jerusalem, so will my wrath
> be poured out on you when you go to Egypt.
> (Jeremiah 42:18)
> Remnant of Judah, the Lord has told you, "Do not go
> to Egypt." (Jeremiah 42:19)

As nuanced and cryptic as this message may initially
appear to be, its central theme is Don't. Go. To. Egypt.

Easy enough. After years of evidence about what happens when they disobey God, Israel can clearly see they
really only have one option here.

> Azariah son of Hoshaiah and Johanan son of Kareah
> and all the arrogant men said to Jeremiah, "You are
> lying! The Lord our God has not sent you to say, 'You
> must not go to Egypt to settle there.'"…So they
> entered Egypt in disobedience to the Lord. (Jeremiah
> 43:2, 7)

The fact that things didn't go well in Egypt was probably
as shocking to Jeremiah as your friend's "So, the life coaching thing didn't pan out and he just sits around and plays
video games all day" was to you.

It's easy to pick on people for their blind spots, but we are all susceptible to the *What happened to them won't happen to me* school of thought.

Some of this optimism is good and necessary. We certainly don't need to be paralyzed by other people's failures. But (as "all the arrogant men" could tell you), blind arrogance is equally as dangerous. Great value lies in stories of those who have gone before us. Lessons to learn. Wisdom to glean.

None of us are guaranteed the success others have had, and none of us are immune from the mistakes others have made.

And, as a general rule, in my opinion, we should take with a grain of salt anyone aspiring to be a life coach. Coaching that doesn't require a whistle is suspect.

Get Curious

What can you learn from a time when someone close to you experienced success? What can you learn from a time when someone close to you experienced failure?

The Cloak and the Spit

After he took him aside, away from the crowd,
Jesus put his fingers into the man's ears.
Then he spit and touched the man's tongue.

MARK 7:33

Having a job where they provide coffee in the break room is great. Having a job where they provide *good* coffee is even better. Going to a baseball game is great. Going to a baseball game with tickets for good seats is even better. Getting an eight-count of Chick-fil-A nuggets is great. Getting nine nuggets in your eight-count box of nuggets is even better.

None of the above scenarios is bad. Everyone's "winning" in a sense. Some just win by a greater margin of victory than others.

Jesus made paralyzed people walk, mute people talk, and blind people see. Incredible stuff. Anyone who was the beneficiary of his awesome power was beyond blessed. It's just...some were a little more blessed than others.

With Jesus, we see two primary methods for healing. The first one involved Jesus' cloak.

Wherever he went—into villages, towns or countryside—they placed the sick in the marketplaces. They begged him to let them touch even the edge of his cloak, and all who touched it were healed. (Mark 6:56)

Seems sanitary enough. The second method was a little less so, as it involved Jesus' spit.

After he took him aside, away from the crowd, Jesus put his fingers into the man's ears. Then he spit and touched the man's tongue. He looked up to heaven and with a deep sigh said to him, "Ephphatha!" (which means "Be opened!"). (Mark 7:33–34)

Listen, when a blind person can see, I don't think they care how their healing happens. Jesus could have rubbed tapioca pudding on their faces and they'd be just as thrilled with the result. I also think that if the spit people heard about the tapioca people, they'd probably think, "You know, that wouldn't have been too bad…"

We should all recognize this feeling. Someone at work experiences immediate and tremendous success when you've been toiling at it for years. Your friend's kid gladly eats anything set in front of him, but your offspring prefers to survive on animal crackers and frozen waffles. Someone in your circle experiences healing and restoration in a battle against addiction, but you can't seem to gain any meaningful ground.

These "must be nice" moments are familiar. Everyone we interact with is "better off" than us in some way, if that's the truth we're looking to find. When these emotions start to creep in, it's critical to ground ourselves in the truth that the path before us is the right one for us, the best one for us. We

believe in a God who is powerful enough to do the impossible and personal enough to intimately care about each and every one of our situations.

God always makes a way for us, different as those ways may be. And the way always leads toward redemption and restoration.

Next time someone gets that promotion and you do not, or someone forms an ideal relationship and you don't, or someone gets an extra nugget in their meal, remember that God sees you, loves you, and you can thrive on the path before you.

Plus, that extra nugget is mostly breading anyway.

Get Curious

Do you find yourself more grateful for what you have or more slighted by the life you live? Would you approach anything differently if you believed that where you are is where you are meant to be?

A Matter of Perspective

They knew he was running away from the LORD,
because he had already told them so.

JONAH 1:10

I once had an idea for a tattoo. It was big, complicated, full of metaphorical imagery, and I thought it was so brilliant that I had to tell my wife. As I heard myself talking about it and watched the ever-increasingly inquisitive look on her face, I realized, "This tattoo idea is not good. This is, in fact, a very bad idea for a tattoo."

I don't remember every detail about the tattoo, but I do know it involved a storm, a particular number of stars, a broken Roman soldier's helmet, I think an Italian and Israeli flag were involved somehow, and stop laughing. I already acknowledged it wasn't a good idea.

An outside perspective is tremendously helpful to our thought process. We can spend hours and days and weeks tinkering with an idea, molding it, shaping it, refining it, and then end up so close to it that we can no longer see it for what it really is.

The trick is, we have to actually listen to this trusted advisor we're consulting with or, in my case, just look at my wife's face. This is where Jonah messed up.

They knew he was running away from the LORD,
because he had already told them so. (Jonah 1:10)

This passage tells us that Jonah said, out loud, that he was getting on a boat to go to another town (Tarshish) *to run away from God.* We don't have details on the conversation, so I've fleshed out how I believe it probably sounded between Jonah his fellow boat passenger:

Jonah: So, are you just visiting Tarshish, or is that where you live?

Gayle: My daughter just gave birth and I'm going to meet my grandbaby.

Jonah: Wow, that's great.

Gayle: Yeah! What about you?

Jonah: Oh, God told me to go do something I didn't want to do, so I'm running away.

Gayle: You don't say.

Jonah: Yep.

Gayle: I'm sorry, I'm not super religious, but can this God of yours not see people who are on boats?

Jonah: Haha, of course. God can see everything.

Gayle: But…God doesn't go to Tarshish, though?

Jonah: No, God can go wherever God wants.

Gayle: How does this end up with you escaping God?

Jonah: You don't get it.

Gayle: I'm just curiou—

Jonah: It's bright out here. I'm going to sit in the shade.

Jonah was shocked at how the rest of his story played out. Gayle was probably less shocked.

This is the power of perspective. Jonah was loaded with all kinds of personal feelings toward the Ninevites, and they had started to cloud his thoughts on everything, including his thoughts on God. Gayle had no fish in the fight.

Whatever it is we're processing—a romantic relationship, a passion project, a family situation, a work problem—an outsider's perspective can be a critical asset, as long as we take the time to listen to and consider their insight.

Find your "Gayle" and listen to what she says when you discuss your plan. Otherwise, you may end up vomited out on the shore by a fish.

Which kind of sounds like a cool idea for a tattoo, am I right?

Get Curious

Do you seek out the opinion of good
friends or family on personal matters?
Do you truly listen to their assessments
and take their opinions seriously?
Do you seek God's perspective?

It Could Be Worse

*My lord the king should not be concerned
about the report that all the king's sons
are dead. Only Amnon is dead.*

2 SAMUEL 13:33

In today's modern world full of technological marvels, communication can still be difficult. Between spotty reception, frozen FaceTime calls, and iMessages that tell you they sent as regular messages but never actually sent at all, it's amazing we get any points across to each other.

So many of today's successful communication attempts are attributed to emojis. Emojis are like a modern take on the cave drawings of old. Simple images used to convey deep and important meaning. An appropriately crafted emoji string leaves little room for misinterpretation.

While ambiguous tone and spelling errors may interrupt more primitive forms of communication, a sushi emoji/thumbs-up emoji/praise hands emoji combo transmits an airtight message. Right?

If we have this technology available to us and yet still occasionally have a hard time communicating, imagine the world before all these wondrous innovations. Your mind is probably drifting back to a time of fax machines, beepers, and the iPhone 2s. But there was a time even before that when mobile communication was so bad it led to mistakes like this:

> While they were on their way, the report came to David: "Absalom has struck down all the king's sons; not one of them is left." The king stood up, tore his clothes and lay down on the ground; and all his attendants stood by with their clothes torn. But Jonadab son of Shimeah, David's brother, said, "My lord should not think that they killed all the princes; only Amnon is dead." (2 Samuel 13:30–32)

I can't say exactly how, but I'm certain autocorrect is to blame for this confusion.

What a tough position King David is in here. There's certainly a sense of relief that the news is not as bad as it first appeared to be (that first news was Job-like), but still an obvious reason for grief.

This unfortunate tension is a sensation I've seen people inflict on themselves or have inflicted on them by well-meaning members of their community. It comes through sentiments like, "It could be worse," or "Imagine if <insert an even more awful thing> had happened." I understand that people want to ease suffering and help in some way. But much like that one random guy in all your meetings or the phrase "agree to disagree," these *comforts* don't contribute anything helpful. The sentiments can even be hurtful.

While usually delivered with the best of intentions, they can suggest that the grief experienced is unnecessary or overblown. Comparing reality with more tragic, hypothetical

realities can belittle the very real, very painful experience of the person grieving.

Whatever you're feeling as you work through a difficult moment, circumstance, or season of life, you are entitled to feel it. No amount of "more" difficult or devastating situations will alleviate the hurt in your situation. Just because the worst didn't happen doesn't mean whatever happened wasn't painful. Give yourself the space to process through it, feel it, and take your time. Don't let anyone devalue the difficulty of your process by comparing it to a different one.

And as you do that, I want to encourage you with the clearest and most heartfelt language I know.

Cat shedding single tear emoji/Heart emoji/Strong arm emoji.

Get Curious

Is there anything you need to work through that you've been putting off? Have you given yourself ample permission to process your experiences?

Weird Turns or Wrong Turns?

One of the company of the prophets said to his companion, "Strike me with your weapon," but he refused. So, the prophet said, "Because you have not obeyed the LORD, as soon as you leave me a lion will kill you."

1 KINGS 20:35–36

I'm not sure if Google Maps knows we are rivals, but we are. When Google Maps gives me an ETA, I set out immediately to defeat it. When it suggests a route for me, I instinctively resist. I'll note the recommended course of direction and think, *Oh, I can get there much quicker than this. I can streamline this whole route.* Then I laugh at the superiority of the human brain over the machine and wonder why we were ever concerned that computers would take over the world.

Forty-five minutes into being stuck behind an accident on my alternate route, I start to think that the *Terminator* franchise may have been on to something.

Just because directions don't seem right doesn't necessarily mean they are wrong. This is particularly true when it pertains to God. People in the Bible received some pretty strange directions. Most of the time, the instructions were followed and the result was good. Like when Elisha tells a man with leprosy to take a bath in the Jordan River seven times and he's healed. (2 Kings 5), or when God tells the Israelites to power-walk around a fortified city a bunch of times and then the walls of the city crumble (Joshua 6).

Other times, the instructions were not followed, and the results were less than ideal.

> By the word of the LORD one of the company of the prophets said to his companion, "Strike me with your weapon," but he refused. So the prophet said, "Because you have not obeyed the LORD, as soon as you leave me a lion will kill you." And after the man went away, a lion found him and killed him. (1 Kings 20:35–36)

I don't know if I could bring myself to hit someone even if they asked me, which is why my career as a blackjack dealer stalled so quickly.

We love to make plans and attempt to measure incremental progress on our way toward our goals, but that's not always the way the God of the Bible works. Track Joseph's path to becoming prime minister of Egypt. Joseph is thrown in a well, then he's sold into slavery, then he's wrongly convicted and sentenced to jail, then he's the second most powerful person in the world (Genesis 37–41). These are not the traditional rungs on the ladder of success.

While it may seem like circumstances you're dealing with are only inhibiting you from fulfilling your purpose, these perceived hindrances may very well be necessary steps on the path God is leading you down. We seldom have all the information and, usually, the information we have goes only as far as the next right thing. Go wash in this river. Walk around this city. We will end up where we are supposed to end up if we follow these strange directions, one step at a time.

God's way is not always the most direct way, but it is the right way. Any attempt to circumvent the suggested route leaves us stuck in traffic and wondering what we can do to get on Siri's good side…you know…just in case.

Get Curious

Do you trust that God is making a way for you to live out the purpose of your life? Do you believe that the moment you're in is a step on the way to fulfilling your purpose? What is your next right thing?

Road Trip Energy

Jesus was in the stern, sleeping on a cushion.
The disciples woke him and said to him,
"Teacher, don't you care if we drown?"

MARK 4:38

I love road trips. I love listening to the radio or a passenger-seat DJ or random mixtape CDs I made fifteen years earlier. I love stopping for gas and getting snacks and wondering exactly how disgusting the bathroom's going to be. I love honking the horn excessively when we cross a state line. It's. All. The. Best.

I feel an obligation to drive on road trips. I once drove a car full of my friends from Alabama all the way back to Florida after attending a college football game. One time I drove our family around Maine in a rented RV, and other than the part where I bumped it into the side of a bridge and when I closed my eyes as I pulled out of a tight parking situation, I drove that monstrosity like a pro.

It's from this place that I ponder the story of Jesus, the disciples, and the storm. Jesus had been leading the disciples around traveling, teaching, healing, upsetting the sociopolitical order of the day, and they were all understandably worn out. Jesus recommended that they recharge with a boating retreat (Mark 4:35), and away they went.

At some point on the journey, Jesus lay down for a nap.

While there may be nuanced differences between nautical and automobile travel, I imagine a conversation similar to the ones I've experienced ensued.

> Disciples: Hey, Jesus, why don't you go down below
>   and close your eyes for a minute?
> Jesus: No, I'm okay. I want to be sure we keep moving.
> Disciples: Don't sweat it. We've got everything under
>   control here.
> Jesus: Are you sure?
> Disciples: Yes, absolutely. You go get some rest.
> Jesus: Okay, just keep your hands at 10 and—
> Disciples: We've got it.

Jesus headed down below the ship and, as I imagine it, had just fallen into deep REM sleep when a storm rolled in.

> The disciples woke him and said to him, "Teacher,
> don't you care if we drown?" (Mark 4:38)

This is what happens when you let someone else drive.

Jesus shut down the storm with all the tact one uses to address an obnoxiously barking dog, and the disciples were left to reconsider exactly who it was they were dealing with (Mark 4:39–41).

The gospel of Jesus Christ, the good news that God loves us and has made a way for redemption is something we need all the time. This desperate need for the gospel makes me uncomfortable, quite frankly, because I feel obligated to drive. I don't want to be a burden. I don't want to be this needy all the time, but the gospel is good enough,

big enough, and powerful enough to meet my substantial need.

Several of the disciples were fishermen by trade, and Jesus was a carpenter. Did they think then, as I sometimes do now, *Jesus, you can take it easy, I'm actually a little bit more familiar with this thing. I got it from here*?

We need to remain constantly grounded in the gospel if we are ever to fulfill the most important of our aspirations— to be kind, patient, forgiving, gracious, loving, like Christ. Our need for the gospel never diminishes, and neither does its ability to provide.

Like Cracker Barrel on a road trip, it's always there, right when we need it.

Get curious

Are you fully the person you want to be?
Do you think you can get there
without God?

ThE CoW KinG

He was driven away from people and ate grass like the ox. His body was drenched with the dew of heaven until his hair grew like the feathers of an eagle and his nails like the claws of a bird.

DANIEL 4:33

Backup quarterback is the best job in the world. They make more money than most doctors, have very little risk of getting hurt, and they're a constant symbol of hope to the fans—hope that, when the starting QB plays poorly, there's a plan B.

Sometimes that hope is realized. Tom Brady was once a backup before he went on to win all the Super Bowls. Many times, your backup is the equivalent of a bald spare tire. Yes, you technically *can* drive on it, but it's uncomfortable and dangerous and you'd be wise to get your real tire fixed ASAP.

Which makes me wonder, just how bad was King Nebuchadnezzar's backup? King Nebuchadnezzar was king until he went crazy, and not like "long rant on Facebook about how lizard people run the world" crazy. *Real* crazy.

He was driven away from people and ate grass like the ox. His body was drenched with the dew of heaven until his hair grew like the feathers of an eagle and his nails like the claws of a bird. (Daniel 4:33)

The quarterback equivalent here is that every time they snap you the ball, you pop it, cut it up, and try to eat it. You're not just bad at your job. You're a lunatic.

According to the Bible, this was all part of a lesson God was teaching Nebuchadnezzar about humility. Seven years later, Nebuchadnezzar learns his lesson, and his sanity is restored.

All of which I can make sense of, but what doesn't make sense to me is this:

> At the same time that my sanity was restored…*my advisers and nobles sought me out*, and I was restored to my throne. (Daniel 4:36, emphasis mine)

How bad does the replacement have to be before the advisers and nobles think to themselves, *It's time to bring back the guy who thinks he's a cow?*

It goes to show that no matter how far off the deep end we think things have gone, God is always working out a story of redemption. God's desire for redemption is so much stronger than ours.

My dad was an alcoholic. Nearly every childhood memory I had with him was a painful one. We saw little of each other until a few years ago, when my dad called to ask if we could have lunch together.

He apologized for the way he had lived his life. At that moment, he'd been sober for two months. He stayed sober more than two hundred consecutive days that year. He got to know his grandsons. I was initially cautious about warming up to him, but we sat together at church on Father's Day and

I started to cry. I was living in an unbelievable reconciliation moment and was overwhelmed.

I had given up on my dad, but God had not.

My dad died of a heart attack later that fall. Part of me wondered, *Why?* Why that good season right there at the end? The answer? God simply never stops redeeming. It's a perpetual state. It's the nature of God.

Whenever you think something in your life is too far gone to be fixed, remember my dad, remember Nezzy taking the Chick-fil-A dress-like-a-cow-day thing way too far, and remember there is always reason for hope.

Get Curious

What in your life feels too broken
to be fixed? Have you given up?
Do you still believe God can restore it?

About the Author

ANTHONY RUSSO grew up memorizing Scripture—partly inspired to understand God's Holy Word, but probably more motivated by his pursuit of badges for his Awana vest. He also loves comedy. He's been performing comedy since he was fifteen years old, and did his first nationwide comedy tour at age seventeen. He is the Creative Director and Director of Online Ministry at Calvary Church in Clearwater, Florida, and performs comedy on the internet and all over the country through The Bible is Funny and Isaac Improv. He and his wife, Rachael, live in Seminole, Florida, and have two children. See more on Instagram and YouTube @thebibleisfunny @isaacimprov.